SELF-DEFENSE TECHNIQUES & TACTICS

JOSEPH B. WALKER

HUMAN KINETICS

Library of Congress Cataloging-in-Publication Data

Walker, Joseph (Joseph B.), 1956-
  Self-defense techniques & tactics / Joseph Walker.
     p. cm.
Includes index.
  ISBN 0-7360-3775-6 (pbk.)
  1. Self-defense—Handbooks, manuals, etc. I. Title: Self-defense
techniques and tactics. II. Title.
  GV1111 .W19 2003
  613.6'6—dc21

                        2002153241

ISBN: 0-7360-3775-6

Production Editor: Melinda Graham; **Assistant Editor:** John Wentworth; **Copyeditor:** Barbara Walsh; **Proofreader:** Jennifer L. Davis; **Indexer:** Gerry Messner; **Graphic Designer:** Robert Reuther; **Art and Photo Manager:** Dan Wendt; **Cover Designer:** Keith Blomberg; **Photographer (cover):** Dan Wendt; **Photographer (interior):** pages 5, 17, and 168, © ImageState; page 173, Marilyn Newton, Reno Gazette-Journal; all other photos by Tom Roberts; **Printer:** United Graphics

Human Kinetics books are available at special discounts for bulk purchase. Special editions or book excerpts can also be created to specification. For details, contact the Special Sales Manager at Human Kinetics.

Printed in the United States of America

10 9 8 7 6 5 4 3 2 1

Human Kinetics
Web site: www.HumanKinetics.com

United States: Human Kinetics, P.O. Box 5076, Champaign, IL 61825-5076, 800-747-4457, e-mail: humank@hkusa.com

Canada: Human Kinetics, 475 Devonshire Road Unit 100, Windsor, ON N8Y 2L5, 800-465-7301 (in Canada only), e-mail: orders@hkcanada.com

Europe: Human Kinetics, 107 Bradford Road, Stanningley, Leeds LS28 6AT, United Kingdom +44 (0) 113 255 5665, e-mail: hk@hkeurope.com

Australia: Human Kinetics, 57A Price Avenue, Lower Mitcham, South Australia 5062, 08 8277 1555, e-mail: liahka@senet.com.au

New Zealand: Human Kinetics, P.O. Box 105-231, Auckland Central, 09-523-3462, e-mail: hkp@ihug.co.nz

I dedicate this book to my loving family. To my daughters, Ellyn, Alyssa, Bethany, Samantha, and Paige—may you always stay safe. You forever have all of my love. To my darling wife, Coleen—you have given me the courage to never give up. I love you. And to my mother and father—thank you for making me the person I am today.

CONTENTS

FOREWORD

Over my 35 years of martial arts training, I have been involved with many motion pictures, authored four books, and won more than 300 international karate championships. This book, *Self-Defense Techniques & Tactics,* is the very first book that I recommend to everyone, from novices to studious martial artists. Read this book and incorporate it into your daily lives. I am impressed by Joseph Walker's ability to articulate and illustrate these self-defense techniques in a way that is simple and easy to understand. I believe this book will help all readers emerge victorious from their self-defense encounters.

I want to reiterate the key concept that Walker emphasizes throughout this book: Self-defense is just what the term implies—the defense of one's self. These are not techniques to use in an offensive manner. Please pass this book on to your friends and loved ones; the information it contains is critical to survival in today's world. I hope this book inspires readers to take their training to the next level.

And as for you, Joe—I am eagerly awaiting your future work.

GRAND MASTER (PASTOR) DR. DONNIE WILLIAMS
1977 INTERNATIONAL KARATE CHAMPION

PREFACE

Practicing self-defense is like preparing to take a road trip. Before leaving home, we study the map so we know as much as possible about how to get where we are going, as well as alternate routes to take in case of unforeseen circumstances. Think of this book as a kind of road map to self-defense. Through careful and consistent study of self-defense, you can learn the tactics and individual components, practice the movements of self-defense techniques, and be able to apply them in altercations.

The founding members of kifaru jitsu martial arts, the basis on which this system of self-defense is founded, are all senior master instructors who have significant experience as law enforcement officials and have worked diligently to overcome the efforts of criminals who seek to cause harm. The techniques in this system are designed to expeditiously stop the assailant by means of delivering effective physical control. Control can take the form of pain compliance (the amount of pain used to compel an aggressor to be noncombative), complete incapacitation of the aggressor, or rendering the aggressor unconscious.

Each technique is based on common sense and economy of motion and borrows from a variety of martial arts systems those movements that are most effective in expeditiously stopping any attack. These techniques always involve a combination of moves, not just one movement. The first move is usually a block, evasive move, or strike, followed by a series of strikes designed to quickly incapacitate the assailant. Also, each strike is designed to augment the one that preceded it as well as set up subsequent strikes. In an assault by someone who is armed, effective self-defense techniques result in immediate control of the weapon and incapacitation of the assailant.

This book presents many techniques to use in self-defense. All of the movements illustrated could result in death or serious bodily injury to the assailant. Therefore, long before you find yourself in an attack situation, do enough research to ensure self-defense safcty—not only physically, but legally as well. Doing this research before entering any type of confrontation will give you confidence that employing the techniques is justified to stop an attack or hinder an attacker from inflicting further harm.

During my law enforcement career, I have had many encounters with violent offenders. With the proper use of tactics, these offenders were overwhelmed not by brute force but by the finesse of technique. Training in this system has kept me out of harm's way and given me the skills to physically defeat violent offenders who choose to physically resist an armed law enforcement officer.

This book is designed to educate anyone wishing to become more adept at self-defense. My goal is to give the reader useful information on what to do before, during, and after any attack to reduce the potential for harm and to emerge from the encounter unscathed. If an attack cannot be avoided, someone who knows what could happen during all stages of an encounter and has prepared in advance for the best- and worst-case scenarios will have the greatest chance of success.

Topics this book covers include physical techniques to defend against hand strikes, kicks, and weapons and street crimes such as car jacking, armed robbery, and kidnapping. A step-by-step approach details each attack situation and the appropriate technique to counter the attack. Throughout the chapters I illustrate physical techniques and mental tactics that have been proven to work in combat.

This book will enlighten people to the kind of dangers that exist in today's society, illustrate various techniques and tactics that can be used effectively against predators, and provide the confidence you need to get through nearly any violent encounter.

Stay alive and safe!

ACKNOWLEDGMENTS

First, I thank Jesus Christ, my Lord and Savior. Without his hand in my life, God only knows where I'd be. Second, I want to thank my primary martial arts instructors, Stanford McNeal and Alexander Archie. I also have great appreciation and thanks for Steve Muhammad and Donnie Williams, two grand masters who have shown me the other side of the equation. All these people have significantly shaped the course of my life. I would also like to thank all my martial artist friends and family—Ross Beiggs, Steve Hurd, and Eddie Solis—who took me in as a snotty-nosed kid and helped me develop into a national champion. Last, I'd like to acknowledge my memories of Larry Sir Mons and Chip Steen, two men who gave me time when I most needed it.

1

ESSENTIALS OF PERSONAL DEFENSE

Physical self-defense occurs when someone being attacked evades or stops an assailant by launching effective counterstrikes to deter further attack. The defender never initiates an act of aggression and uses movements that are totally defensive in nature and application. Self-defense is used when a person is about to be or is being attacked and needs to take immediate action to avoid sustaining significant injury. It is within this definition that self-defense techniques operate.

SELF-DEFENSE TODAY

Self-defense is different today than it was 30 or 40 years ago. Today, fights occur commonly at athletic contests, bars, parties, and even on the interstate, when drivers get frustrated enough to stop their vehicles and come to blows. In the past, such fights were most likely skirmishes or scuffles; today, there's never any telling who has a weapon and is ready to use it. More people than ever—from violent criminals to enraged spectators—are likely to inflict bodily harm or death. The young, brutal criminals of today are not satisfied with mere burglary or breaking and entering. Often, instead of fleeing when caught in the act, they turn violent. Instead of taking only money or property, they take a life. Guns and knives have never been more accessible to criminals. In fact, you're best off assuming every person you meet has a weapon. Otherwise, you might be caught off guard.

Even when weapons are not used, today's fights can be extremely dangerous. A person who knocks someone to the ground during a fight might continue to deliver devastating strikes regardless of the reason for the fight and without considering the amount of force used. Enraged attackers have been known to continue delivering kicks and blows even when their victim has lost consciousness. Frustration, stress, and the potential for rage plague our society. We have never lived in more dangerous times.

The days of the fair fight are over. Weapons might be introduced at any stage of an altercation. An assailant either brings a weapon and uses it to overwhelm a victim, or he improvises one (such as a rock, stick, or bottle found nearby) if he feels incapable of winning the fight. Sometimes, after a fight has ended, an assailant may return to the scene with a weapon as a means of retribution. In any case, today's street-fighting assailants do not employ what were once known as "fair" tactics. Defenders should assume that the fight will not be fair, that a number of assailants might attack at once, and that they might use deadly weapons.

Those who want to succeed in defending any type of attack should learn self-defense techniques that represent various disciplines, combining punching and kicking with throwing and grappling. Building a repertoire of techniques for use in a variety of altercations gives you the best shot for safety. The well-rounded defender must be capable of defending against any attack, whether it be a punch, a kick, ground fighting (grabbing and wrestling to the ground), or the use of an improvised weapon.

A defender must be prepared to respond to an attack psychologically as well as physically. Understanding how and why an assailant moves in a particular fashion and what motivates such a person will enable the defender to include more tools in his or her self-defense arsenal. Today's defender must understand that self-defense entails awareness, prevention, and the actual physical moves to be used in self-defense. The assailant will psychologically challenge the defender, who must be fully in control of his or her emotional response to any perceived threat. Mental control is essential if the defender is to develop and implement an efficient, effective response to any threat, whether that response takes the form of de-escalation or a physical action. With diligent self-defense practice, the defender will develop acute observation skills that will enable him or her to notice the verbal and nonverbal cues that precede an assailant's attack. The bottom line is always that the defender must be fully capable of defending against a physical attack.

STUDYING MARTIAL ARTS

If you want to study with a martial arts instructor, shop around for the school and instructor that best fit your needs. Do not just sign up with the largest school in the area or the first one listed in the yellow pages. Visit the school; watch the classes; and evaluate the level of proficiency of the instructor, the top students, and the intermediate and beginning students. Stay away from schools that do not allow prospective students to watch several classes and that claim to guard their "secret" material. Avoid schools where students are routinely and carelessly injured during their training through either the students' or instructor's lack of control. And watch out for "diploma mills" that churn out black belts as fast as burgers at a fast-food joint. These types of schools typically promote students who are willing to pay for further instruction (known as "buying the black belt") but are not necessarily physically competent to defend themselves in spontaneous situations.

Training should require a certain level of physical conditioning and a degree of cardiovascular fitness, but not at the expense of proper technique. Students should learn techniques that will disable an attacker, not exercise themselves to death. Classes that contain more physical exercise than martial arts self-defense techniques usually indicate that the instructor isn't skilled in or comfortable teaching self-defense techniques and tactics, or that the focus has moved away from martial arts techniques and toward aerobics.

A person need not be in top physical shape to be a successful defender, but maintaining a certain level of fitness helps the mind and body adapt to the ever-changing tactical and environmental challenges that arise during an altercation. And in the event that an injury occurs during training or an altercation, a person who is physically fit will recover faster than someone who is not.

A martial arts class that emphasizes self-defense should adequately cover empty-hand defenses against single or multiple opponents as well as defense against weapons. The aggressor may attack from any angle with either hand or foot, or with a weapon such as a rock, a brick, a stick, a bottle, brass knuckles, a knife, or a gun. If the instructor has no idea what to do when faced with an armed assailant other than run away or surrender, look for another instructor.

This is not to suggest that a defender should always resist an armed assailant. If the opportunity exists to escape the situation, do so. If the assailant merely wants your property, handing it over may be the best way to escape harm. But some assailants want to cause physical harm, and the instructor should be capable of teaching techniques and tactics to use in that extremely dangerous situation and ensure that the techniques and tactics use realistic strategies.

Some martial arts schools emphasize "streetwise" techniques, whereas others focus on "traditional" or "competition" movements. When visiting a school, ask the instructor which techniques are taught and what the emphasis of instruction is. The instructor, as well as the advanced and intermediate students, should be able to execute the techniques. Observe the movements from a safe distance. Evaluate not only the instructor but the students as well. Does the instructor appear to be competent and move fluidly? Are the students capable of performing the techniques the instructor is teaching them? Is safety incorporated into the practice sessions so students do not needlessly injure one another?

Take a look at the school's enrollment policy. Be skeptical of a school that has an inflexible contract or that requires more than a one-year obligation. Sometimes things happen in life that may preclude any lengthy contractual agreement. Job promotions, family considerations, and other factors may sometimes interfere with consistent training. Ensure that if you need to suspend training for unforeseen emergencies, the contract has provisions to allow it.

ELEMENTS OF SELF-DEFENSE

Self-defense does not mean just the physical ability to defend against an attack. One of the most essential elements in self-defense is awareness. A defender should be capable of detecting a problem before taking physical action. Self-defense includes the ability to observe, evaluate, and choose a particular course of action to maximize safety.

Three main elements are present in personal safety: the victim or defender, the location, and the aggressor. The more components the defender is able to control, the greater the chances of survival.

VICTIM OR DEFENDER

The first element is the victim or defender. Whatever the potential victim does first—whether it is avoiding or escaping from the situation during the beginning stages of the attack, or taking the appropriate action toward the attacker once the attack has begun—will have a direct bearing on whether he or she survives the attack. Self-defense tactics and training play a significant role in this element.

To obtain and maintain competency in self-defense, the defender should physically and mentally rehearse an attack situation many times before any real attack occurs. The purpose of the rehearsal is to work through the rough spots so that when the moment of truth finally comes, any attack can be overcome. In some situations, a physical altercation may be avoidable; the defender may need only to take evasive action to avoid a violent encounter. In other cases, a defender may have no choice but to become involved in a physical altercation. When forced to take physical action, the defender should use self-defense techniques without hesitation to stop the assailant from causing any physical harm.

LOCATION OF THE ATTACK

The second element is the location of the attack. The attack may occur within either the defender's or the assailant's environment, usually in a place chosen by the assailant. Defenders can do certain things to increase their safety in their own environment. This is known as *target hardening*. Target hardening also refers to employing measures to reduce the risk of an area being exploited. A home can be target hardened by ensuring that doors and windows are locked, exterior lighting is equipped with motion-sensor lights, and an alarm system installed by a reputable company is in place.

To target harden a vehicle, keep the doors locked and windows rolled up. Being aware of and avoiding high-crime areas of a city may keep the defender from becoming a potential victim. Often, "danger signs" within a location—something that just does not look right or feel right, or the lack of something that should be present—are clues that something bad is about to take place. One example of a danger sign is a person wearing a large coat in a warm environment; the coat is possibly concealing an illegal handgun. Some people who see these signs don't understand their importance and simply ignore them. A defender can learn, however, to pay close attention to the environment and the people within it. Whenever danger signals are present, the defender must take immediate action to maximize safety. Failing to do so can lead to a deterioration of the situation to the point that violence erupts and escaping the situation safely is no longer an option.

Any location can be dangerous. Be aware of your surroundings.

The Aggressor

The last of these three elements is the aggressor, the element over which the defender will usually have the least amount of control or influence. The aggressor will have a specific motive and a victim in mind and will choose the location and the time to begin the attack. A verbal assault may precede the physical altercation, or the aggressor may elect to violently attack without any verbal warning. The only way a potential victim may have any influence over this element is to use an evasive tactic (if possible) or to physically resist the attack. If the defender's counterattack is sufficient, the aggressor's violence will stop. An effective counterattack will also psychologically impact the aggressor. The aggressor may feel that he or she underestimated the potential victim and may want to escape from the vicious and relentless counterattack. When dealing with a mentally hardened aggressor, the defender must use a physical technique that is sure to incapacitate any further act of aggression.

Demeanor

When the defender is initially approached by the aggressor, the defender's body posture must be nonthreatening to the aggressor. If the defender's posture indicates an offensive demeanor, the aggressor may interpret this as an invitation to a physical altercation. While displaying a nonthreatening demeanor, the defender must also be mentally and physically prepared to meet the aggressor's attack.

Defenders should never fold their arms across their chest, place their hands behind their back or in their pockets, or interlace their fingers. All these positions are detrimental to the defender in that they do not facilitate any defense for blocking an attack. However, the defender should never assume any type of fighting stance in anticipation of an attack from the aggressor. If the aggressor interprets any movement by the defender as fighting preparedness, especially if the defender exhibits any proficiency in fighting skills, the aggressor may escalate the violence to a much more serious level than that initially intended. The defender should stand about 10 feet from the assailant and at a slight angle, with feet no more than shoulder-width apart and hands free of obstacles and available for blocking, deflecting, or striking.

Throughout the episode, the defender should be aware of exactly how far away the aggressor is. Standing too close to the attacker will inhibit any effective defense. Right away, it is imperative that the defender look at the aggressor's hands and waistband to see if there's a weapon—either a conventional type (a club, knife, or gun) or an improvised one (a stick, a rock, or something not intended to be a weapon). If the aggressor is armed, the danger level is critically high and calls for immediate life-

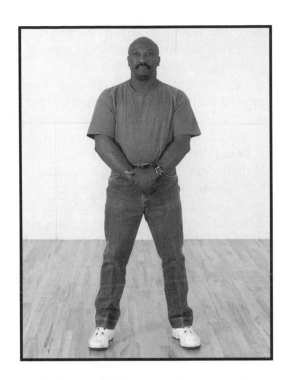

Street-ready position.

saving measures. These measures might include escaping or using a physical technique against an armed aggressor.

A defender who is about to deliver a self-defense strike to the aggressor must refrain from looking directly at the target area. Unless the defender is proficient in self-defense, looking at the intended target is a natural tendency. But doing this can have dangerous consequences; an aggressor who is able to determine a defender's targets will easily be able to block and counter the strikes. Making eye contact with the aggressor may help prevent the defender from telegraphing his or her intended target.

The aggressor may engage the defender in intimidating conversation before an attack. What is actually said is less important than the aggressor's nonverbal cues (see chapter 3). Keep all conversation with an aggressor to a minimum. Conversing with the aggressor will naturally require the defender to listen to what the aggressor says, think about it, formulate a verbal response, and then speak. This process wastes valuable time for the defender and masks the aggressor's attack. Keep your answers short. The emphasis at this point is not on conversing; observing is much more important. The defender should keep a safe distance from the aggressor and limit conversation.

Engaging in action involves undertaking a specific movement or set of movements with the express purpose of keeping the defender safe. A defender who fails to take appropriate action at the right time may suffer personal harm. Actions may range from escaping (running) from an aggressor to physically defending against an attack. In any particular situation, the best action will be those movements that the defender can perform confidently and that have the greatest likelihood for success in ensuring the defender's safety.

If more than one aggressor is present and the altercation has not yet erupted into violence, escaping from the aggressors or using de-escalation tactics may be the best course of action. With multiple aggressors, with each second that passes, the likelihood increases that one or more of them may attack. The greater the number of aggressors, the less time the defender will have to evaluate options. Take the immediate action that is most likely to result in survival. The defender must observe all of the aggressor's verbal and nonverbal signs, interpret them and decide which ones are threatening, and determine an appropriate course of action to maintain safety.

SAFETY ZONE

The *safety zone* is the physical distance between the aggressor and the defender that allows the defender to observe the aggressor's nonverbal signs of attack and still have time to select and implement an appropriate course of action. Once an aggressor approaches, the defender needs to establish the safety zone. The safety zone should be of sufficient distance to keep the assailant from being able to immediately reach out to punch or kick the defender without ample warning—at least 6 to 10 feet. At this distance, the defender will be capable of noticing any aggressive movement and fully able to respond to that movement. The only reason an aggressor breaches the safety zone is to cause bodily harm. This action means an attack is forthcoming.

CRITICAL DISTANCE

Critical distance is a distance narrower than the safety zone. At this distance—approximately two feet—the defender or the aggressor can *easily* strike or be struck. The aggressor will usually step, walk, or leap into critical distance. The manner in which the aggressor moves into critical distance can be a clear indicator of his or her intentions. Never allow any aggressor to stand inside critical distance without taking appropriate action.

SELF-DEFENSE OPTIONS

When an assailant breaches the safety zone and moves into critical distance, the defender has several options.

• **Do absolutely nothing.** If the defender chooses to do nothing, the assailant will move through the safety zone into critical distance, placing the defender in immediate danger of attack. Doing nothing at this

The arrows show the safety zone at approximately 10 feet and the critical distance zone at approximately 2 feet.

distance places the defender in a "perception-reaction" mode. If the aggressor attacks at that close range, the defender can do virtually nothing to prevent the attack from taking place, block the assailant's strikes, or stop the attack once it has begun.

• **Step backward to reestablish the safety zone.** A defender who elects to move backward should do this only once. Repeatedly moving backward forces the defender to perform at least two critical tasks simultaneously: keep track of the assailant's movements and attempt to avoid potential obstacles that may cause loss of balance or divert attention away from the assailant. An assailant who forces a defender backward may choose to attack because the defender's attention is focused on moving away from the assailant, not on the impending attack.

• **Evade the assailant or escape.** Choosing to evade or escape from an assailant is sometimes the best choice in a self-defense situation. The defender may be able to evade the situation by crossing the street to avoid a particular person or escape a assailant by outrunning him or her. A timely escape will place distance between the assailant and the defender.

Running away when not prepared to fight may give the best chance of survival when the odds are stacked against the defender. An extremely important point about choosing to run away is that the defender must physically be capable of outsprinting and outdistancing the assailant. This is important because at any time during an attempted escape, the defender may be forced to physically engage the assailant in a physical fight if escape isn't possible.

The defender must be aware of the environment and should have a plan as to the best escape route to take. Running away with no destination in mind is the same as having no plan. A place with lots of people may be a good destination. If the attack takes place after dark, consider running to a hiding place such as under a parked and unoccupied vehicle or inside shrubs or a dumpster. You may get dirty, but if it accomplishes the goal, it is worth considering.

• **Use de-escalation skills to avoid a physical confrontation.** De-escalation involves talking to the aggressor in hopes of calming him or her and avoiding a physical altercation. Some aggressors actually feel superior to their intended prey and psychologically think they could easily "take" them in a fistfight. To appeal to the aggressor's ego, the defender must appear to be humble to avoid presenting a challenge. This approach requires a significant degree of confidence on the part of the defender. Some people are unwilling to appear "humble" to anyone, and this approach may not work well for them. Remember, the goal of de-escalation is to reduce the tension of the situation without having to resort to a physical altercation. Do not use a loud tone of voice. Speak slowly in a manner that is not argumentative or offensive. Ask what can be done to resolve the issue without resorting to violence. In asking this question, do not insinuate that you're prepared to defend yourself if necessary. Apologize for any misunderstanding; allow the aggressor to think he's in the right. If the aggressor begins to use profanity and call you offensive names, don't allow this to interfere with your intention to defuse the situation.

These verbal tactics might reduce tension and allow the potential altercation to dissolve; however, always be prepared to defend yourself if the aggressor refuses to leave you in peace.

• **Interpret violation of the safety zone as a prelude to an imminent attack**, and strike the assailant as he or she closes the distance and moves into critical distance. A defensive counterstrike is the best option when all signs point to an imminent attack and the defender cannot wait any longer before the aggressor inflicts serious injury.

To the untrained person, this defensive counterstrike may look like an offensive action, because the defender actually initiates the first bodily contact. The defender must observe the aggressor, who is in the process of striking the defender. By observing all the assailant's clues—verbal and nonverbal—the defender perceives that an attack is forthcoming. The defender will have the opportunity to interrupt the attack by striking the aggressor moments before the aggressor's strike can land.

Some self-defense advocates quote some nebulous law that says a defender must always retreat, warn the assailant of their self-defense skills, or let the aggressor strike first before executing any self-defense technique. Nothing could be further from the truth. A defender is not required to retreat from an attack. In certain situations retreat is neither possible nor practical; a defender who is unable to retreat must know that self-defense is legally allowed. And it is completely unnecessary, even foolish, to warn an aggressor, "I'm competent in self-defense, and I'm prepared to defend myself!" Any verbal warning is a serious waste of time and allows the aggressor to gain valuable information about the defender. Warnings inhibit any attempt at self-defense and allow the aggressor to escalate the level of violence.

Keep in mind, however, that the amount of force a defender can use against an assailant must be reasonable to stop the attack, and the defender must stop using force once the assailant's threat has been neutralized. Any unnecessary physical force against an aggressor once the aggressor's attack has ceased may be considered as initiating an attack. The defender may then be viewed by law officials as the "physical assailant" and held liable in subsequent civil and criminal proceedings.

Consider the following scenario of how an aggressor might pick a fight: Chip walks into a fast-food restaurant where several people are standing near the front counter. As a restaurant employee asks to help the next customer, nobody moves for several seconds, giving the appearance that everyone has already been waited on.

Chip then steps up to the counter to place his order. A very loud and boisterous man standing nearby says to Chip, "Hey, I've been standing here waiting to order." Using de-escalation skills, Chip steps aside and apologizes in a friendly way. A minute or two later, Chip places and receives his order. As he begins to leave the restaurant, the boisterous man walks outside and approaches him. "I know you saw me standing there. You butted right in front of me." Chip sees that the man is quite agitated and is rapidly closing in on his critical distance. The man clenches his right hand into a fist and begins to throw a punch at Chip's face. Chip uses a technique consisting of a left outer forearm block and a right strike into the right striking biceps of the aggressor to disable his punching arm. Chips steps into the aggressor with his right foot and delivers a right elbow strike to the aggressor's body. Chip uses a right leg takedown, causing the aggressor to fall onto his backside. Before the aggressor can recover from this fall, Chip delivers a devastating stomp kick to the torso to knock the wind out of the aggressor. Chip then leaves the immediate area and drives to a safe place where he can telephone the police to report the incident and to summon medical assistance to aid the downed aggressor in the restaurant's parking lot.

In this scenario, Chip used de-escalation skills in a volatile situation to no avail. He would not have been capable of escaping without placing himself at great risk. With no other options, Chip took defensive action and used a self-defense technique designed to take the aggressor to the ground.

If Chip had waited a second longer, the delay might have allowed the aggressor to land one or more punches, which could have had devastating effects and negated any attempt Chip might have made at self-defense.

Each situation dictates the best option for self-defense. A defender who has invested time wisely during self-defense training will have the best options to choose from. This defender will have rehearsed tactics and techniques many times before the actual altercation.

GADGETS FOR SELF-DEFENSE

A vast number of gadgets are available on the market for use in self-defense. These include personal alarms, key chains used as striking tools, stun guns, such as the Taser®, and chemical sprays. Most of these gadgets have extremely limited use or practicality. The defender should never rely solely on any marketed tool, despite the number of people who endorse them.

Of all the self-defense tools on the market, the civilian model of the Taser® stun gun offers the best chance for practical application, and misting oil-based pepper sprays are a close second. The stun gun is a less than lethal weapon designed to cause temporary incapacitation. It can shoot two small probes of high-voltage insulated wire up to 15 feet. Before buying these tools, the defender must first know whether local or state laws prohibit their use or possession. Anyone who does purchase one of these tools will need to fully familiarize themselves with it before using it in a real-life situation.

Chemical sprays are available in a range of sizes, strengths, and deployment applications. These sprays can range from a straight stream of liquid (capable of reaching about six feet) to a misting funnel that reaches only about two feet. The defender must know how the agent will be propelled from the canister and the distance at which the spray will be most effective. Before using the spray in an actual situation, shake the canister to mix the agent and propellant while simultaneously checking the wind direction and intensity. Wind and rain will greatly inhibit the application of this tool. The defender should never spray the aggressor in an environment where the wind will return the spray toward the defender. Spray the aggressor in the facial area, concentrating on the eyes, nose, and mouth in two-second bursts. If the aggressor opens his or her eyes or mouth during the application, spray those areas again! After spraying the aggressor, the defender should move to a different position to conceal his or her exact location from the aggressor.

There are some restrictions to the use of pepper spray. If this agent is applied in an enclosed area, or if close physical contact occurs during the encounter, the defender will sustain some residual effects. Never use this agent near an open flame, as the contents are highly flammable. Never leave chemical sprays in a hot automobile; pepper spray canisters have been known to explode and contaminate everything inside the vehicle.

When using a stun gun, deploy the weapon so that both probes strike the assailant's torso. Once the probes make contact, they immediately deliver the voltage into the assailant. During this time, the assailant may fall to the ground. Be prepared to deploy the weapon a second or third time if the assailant begins to rise.

A problem can occur if one of the probes breaks off when the assailant falls to the ground. The assailant may comply while the stun gun is cycling during the five seconds, but after that time has elapsed, he or she may want to physically engage the defender again. Rather than attempt to reload an additional cartridge into the stun gun, be prepared to "touch stun" the assailant. That is, reach in with the stun gun and touch the assailant's body. Whether the gun's cartridge is in or not, the gun will stun the assailant when the trigger is pressed. Moving in to touch the assailant with the stun gun draws the defender closer to the assailant, so this defense warrants extreme caution.

Never depend solely on a tool, gadget, or device as a complete self-defense plan. Heavily depending on a particular tool for self-defense can have devastating results if the tool fails or, worse, falls into the hands of the assailant. Don't get overly relaxed just because you carry a self-defense instrument. Plan for the worst that could happen, including defending yourself against an aggressor who comes at you with your own weapon.

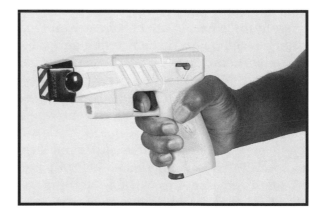

Pepper spray and the Taser® stun gun.

2

MENTAL
READINESS

Self-defense training gives a person the ability to use both physical and mental skills to combat an opponent in a wide range of threatening situations. Self-defense needs to entail not just physical measures but also relevant and logical information that will provide real-life and current information about schemes and methods assailants are using to attack people within their region and across the nation as well.

A *mental model* is a preconceived notion about a particular situation or person. Mental models can be considered stereotypes. For example, certain types of criminals evoke a certain mental picture. An outlaw biker is thought to be a longhaired, unkempt person riding a Harley-Davidson motorcycle. But in reality, not all outlaw bikers dress or look the part. They may wear expensive suits and drive luxury sedans as well as motorcycles. After September 11, 2001, terrorists were envisioned to be Middle Eastern males wearing clothing typical of that part of the world. One look at Richard Reid (a man who resembled a "typical American"), who boarded an American Airlines flight in December 2001 and attempted to ignite an explosive device in his shoe, proved that Americans cannot afford to "profile" how the typical terrorist looks. Look at individual behavior, not just what the person looks like.

We also get mental models burned into our psyches by viewing movies that depict unrealistic self-defense movements. Scenes that show someone evading an oncoming bullet by ducking or bending backward only help to perpetuate these unrealistic mental models.

Many television shows and movies give false impressions of how a fight occurs. Most fight scenes show the aggressor and defender trading blows; often, there is a significant pause between punches or kicks that gives the aggressor or defender a chance to collect himself before the next assault.

In reality, an effective self-defense technique should give the aggressor only one opportunity to initiate an offensive movement. The defender's technique should be immediate and continue relentlessly until the aggressor's violent movement has been completely neutralized. Sometimes the defender may have underestimated the assailant's mental capacity to succeed, and the assailant just does not seem to be deterred. That is why a defender should always have contingency plans that cover *every* conceivable attack an assailant could deploy.

Think about various scenarios of being attacked. Play the "what-if" game. What if an assailant simply refuses to be defeated? What if you are confronted by multiple assailants? Consider the worst-case scenario and make preparations not only to meet but also exceed the challenges of that situation.

Instead of believing mental models that do not necessarily apply to real life, a defender needs to develop a realistic model of appropriate self-defense techniques using appropriate self-defense moves. A single punch or kick will not stop an attack. Defense against an attack should always consist of a technique—a combination of movements strategically designed to enable the defender to block or redirect the incoming strike, move to a position of advantage that will enhance the defender's power, and quickly and effectively deliver multiple counterstrikes to stop the assailant. The rationale for delivering multiple counterstrikes to multiple target areas of the assailant's body is to overwhelm the assailant by inflicting pain over several areas of his or her body instead of just one. The assailant will be incapable of protecting all of the target areas, so strategic placement of these counterstrikes will have an overall devastating effect on the assailant.

STAGES OF AN ATTACK

In just about all attack situations, an aggressor will transition through at least six stages that take place before, during, and after the attack. Knowing these stages and when they will most likely occur will give the defender an opportunity to interrupt the aggressor. In most cases, the following stages will occur either separately or in combination.

SELECTION OF THE VICTIM

The assailant first selects an ideal victim for the attack. To evaluate the chances for a successful attack, the assailant will size up how potential victims carry themselves, their physical appearance, the degree of self-confidence they project, and other nonverbal cues. The largest factor an assailant will consider is whether he or she feels capable of physically and mentally overwhelming the victim. Does the victim appear to be in good shape or capable of defending him- or herself? Is the victim aware of the environment? Can the assailant approach the victim and attack by surprise?

To counter this stage of the attack sequence, a defender must be aware of the environment at all times. This allows the defender to observe potential assailants, note their location, and evaluate escape routes and other defensive strategies. Stay aware of people and suspicious circumstances in the surrounding area. Display an air of confidence that communicates preparedness. This confidence signals potential attackers to choose some other person for a victim. In this stage of the attack, the assailant's perceptions are the main factor, and there may be little a potential victim can do to completely remove the threat.

APPROACH

Next, the assailant will determine how to approach the selected victim. Each assailant will use whatever approach has worked best for them in previous attacks. The assailant may choose a *confidence* approach, using some type of guise to enter the victim's comfort zone in hopes of getting the victim to let his or her guard down. Once this occurs, the assailant will launch the attack. Examples of this are asking for directions, for change for a dollar, or for the time, or any number of other seemingly harmless conversation starters.

If someone approaches and the defender senses the possibility of an attack, take assertive steps to prevent it. Not allowing the person to move inside the safety zone is one important option. If a potential attacker cannot get close enough, he or she will find it very difficult to commit the attack. Also, being aware that the assailant may attempt to lower the defender's guard and refusing to allow that to happen will keep the defender one step ahead. Keep any person who may be a potential attacker at a distance until their intentions are proven.

The other approach an assailant may use is the *blitz*. The blitz attack comes without warning; the assailant suddenly appears, seemingly from nowhere, and uses physical violence to immediately overcome the intended victim. As with the confidence approach, the defender's ability to be acutely aware of the environment is a major defense for any blitz attack. Once the attack begins, the next line of defense is for the defender to immediately and appropriately respond with a self-defense technique. Another defense may also include escaping from the attack. Escaping means more than simply running away. Escape to places where other people are present. Running into an open business, such as a hospital, mall, or store, will likely discourage an attacker.

SELF-DEFENSE TECHNIQUES & TACTICS

INTIMIDATION

The assailant will intimidate the victim to create a credible threat and facilitate the attack. He or she may elect to use physical violence or threats of violence toward either the victim or the victim's loved ones. Keeping the victim in fear of his or her life during the commission of the intended crime greatly increases the assailant's chances of success. For the victim, it is very difficult to keep from being intimidated, at least initially. Intimidation is generally a transition stage; at some point, the actual violence or threats should stop.

When the violence stops and the offender appears to be proceeding to the next stage (the true purpose for the attack), it is imperative that the defender regain control over the attacker's initial mental intimidation and implement his or her self-defense plan. The self-defense plan needs to overcome the attacker's intimidation and totally dominate his mindset.

If it does not appear that the violence will subside, the defender needs to make a conscious decision to immediately employ life-saving measures. For example, if during the intimidation phase the attacker chooses to pound the defender's head into the concrete pavement, the defender cannot afford to wait for the attacker to stop and proceed to the next phase. The defender must immediately employ an effective technique to stop the attacker. In another situation, an attacker wielding a gun or a knife may elect to tell the victim to turn around and get on their knees.

Even when faced with extreme intimidation, the defender should be planning his mode of defense.

This is a classic execution pose, and the attacker will more than likely inflict serious harm as soon as the victim complies. Instead of complying, the defender must employ a self-defense technique to immediately disarm the assailant. Because the attacker is armed with a deadly weapon, the defender has no other viable option to stop the attack than to use a technique that has deadly force.

THE ACT

The assailant will ultimately state, by word or by deed, his or her intention(s) for the attack. The assailant will take a specific action against the victim. If just property is the issue, the assailant may either announce what he or she wants or take the property without saying a word. In this situation, allow the assailant to complete the property crime and leave the scene. If the situation transitions into a personal crime where the assailant is about to cause grave personal harm to the victim, the defender needs to do everything possible to either escape or counteract the violence.

As an example, say the assailant approaches the victim, produces a handgun, and demands money. In this case the victim would be wise to give the assailant the money. Now the assailant repeatedly strikes the victim over the head with the gun, and it appears that the beating will continue. The victim must make a conscious decision to disarm the suspect and employ a technique to neutralize the assailant. Refer to the techniques in chapter 8 for defending against weapons. The defense plan needs to be decisive and cause immediate and significant injury to the assailant. The quicker a defender implements a technique that will incapacitate the assailant, the greater the chance of escape.

PRELUDE TO ESCAPE

Once the act is nearly concluded, the assailant will begin to focus attention on how to escape. If the assailant has not already secured the victim (with handcuffs, duct tape, telephone cords, or the like), he or she may want to do so now. Other means of securing a victim include locking him or her in a room or other confined space (e.g., the trunk of a vehicle, a restaurant cooler) until the assailant can escape.

This is probably one of the most dangerous stages of the entire attack. The assailant may feel that if there are no living witnesses, then the crime will never be solved and they will never be caught. This stage represents a significant risk of personal harm to the victim. Victims in this situation should realize that everything they do or fail to do may have a direct bearing on whether they live or die.

If the victim has not done anything to defend against the attack so far, this may be the last chance to employ a life-saving plan. If the defender is capable of escaping from the assailant, this may be the best choice. Seek the best moment to initiate the escape. The escape may entail not just outrunning the assailant, but hiding until it is safe to emerge. The escape may also involve running into a place where the presence of other people may deter the assailant from attacking further.

ESCAPE

How the assailant flees the scene of the attack depends on the resources available—it may be on foot, in his own vehicle, or in the victim's vehicle. If the assailant is leaving the scene with just property, don't try to stop him. Never chase after an assailant to retrieve personal property. Insurance companies can replace tangible items—but not lives! If an assailant has abducted a loved one, however, do whatever it takes to save the loved one's life. See chapter 9 for information on abductions.

MINDSET FOR
SELF-DEFENSE TRAINING

Effective self-defense requires developing a mental attitude to survive. The proper mental attitude coupled with physical ability will directly affect the outcome of many altercations. The defender must not only develop the body to defend against an attack but must also train the mind to completely defeat an assailant. This attitude is established during self-defense training and must carry over into every physical and mental altercation. The mental effort that training requires can be just as difficult as the physical work.

Develop the mindset necessary to get through whatever course of action is necessary. Some have called this mindset "the zone," defined as the winning attitude to survive. Attitude and physical ability play significant roles in success or failure. Consider the attitude of the hardcore bad guys or gals. These people have decided way in advance that nothing will stop them from getting what they want. Some crime victims are psychologically overwhelmed from the onset of an attack; they feel disbelief that this is actually happening to them. In cases where an assailant uses physical force, it is common for the victim to be psychologically shocked as well as physically stunned from the blows inflicted.

In actual combat, there will always be disparities. The assailant is often significantly taller, heavier, and more muscular than the defender. Because of that significant difference in size, most defenders can initially become intimidated. Assailants come in all shapes, sizes, colors, and states of mental depravity.

As discussed earlier, bad guys and gals can and do look just like anyone else. Once the defender truly understands this concept, the idea of an attack is not so surprising. Consider that this assailant more than likely has an extensive criminal record as well as a criminal mentality that accepts extreme violence as a way of life. This assailant can and will use extreme violence without hesitation to get what he or she wants. Also consider that this assailant has had time to physically and mentally prepare for the attack and has preselected a victim.

Consider that this assailant has likely been incarcerated in some jail, prison, or mental health facility. Most such institutions allow their inmates to use physical exercise as a means of recreation or therapy. Activities such as running, weightlifting, boxing, and wrestling are common. By the time these inmates have been incarcerated for a year or more, they have participated in numerous physical activities and are in great shape when they are released back into society.

Once these hardcore, unrehabilitated offenders are released from their maximum-security vacations, they will be fully prepared to perpetrate their crimes on innocent people and wreak havoc on society until they are once again safely locked away. The defender must be prepared to meet the physical and mental challenges of these attacks. The defender may or may not be capable of changing the circumstances that led to an attack but must be capable of changing the end result of the attack to their favor. Without the proper mental attitude, the defender will be incapable of establishing a winning mindset to overcome the assailant, who has no mental hang-ups about taking property or a life.

One important step in mental readiness is a mental session called *crisis rehearsal*. Sit in a quiet place and imagine an assailant about to attack. Mentally proceed through the steps that lead up to a physical altercation. Notice the adversary's physical demeanor as he or she begins to close the distance from the safety zone into critical distance. At the moment just before the assailant's attack, notice that the intended strike is obvious. See the spontaneous defensive technique being applied to the assailant. Watch the assailant as the counterstrikes reach their intended targets. Observe the assailant being taken to the ground and rendered ineffective by the incapacitating defensive technique.

This type of visualization is important because it helps instill self-confidence and self-image, both an integral part of successful self-defense. Even if the body is capable of rigorous trial, the mind must also be conditioned to stand up to the pressure of an attack.

Take time each week to either read the local newspaper or watch the local television news. There will almost always be a report of a case where some person became a crime victim or was forced into some type of intimidating situation or physical altercation. Envision the situation and think about what the defender may have been capable of doing either to avoid the altercation or to confront the threat directly.

Imagine the mental anguish and intimidation the victim must have experienced, and think about what that person could have done to overcome this act of aggression. Evaluate the type of physical techniques or tactics the victim could have used to defend against the assailant.

Imagine yourself as the victim and examine whether tactics were used incorrectly, and select better options to use in a similar situation. Through careful consideration and hindsight, past performance in situations can almost always be improved. This type of mental replay is not meant to be destructive; people should never beat themselves up over what did occur. Learn from every mistake, and don't make the same mistake twice.

MENTAL CONDITIONS

Crimes occur in nearly every city, and citizens need to be aware of potential dangers as they go about their legitimate business on a daily basis. The risk of an act of violence against innocent people is higher today than a decade ago. People should establish mental conditions to place themselves in a proper mindset when they encounter dangerous situations. When a situation occurs, the defender should take whatever steps are appropriate to alleviate the danger.

Condition Green is a low risk of danger. Given the circumstances, a dangerous situation could arise, but there's nothing dangerous occurring at the time. Condition Blue is a guarded condition, indicating that possible danger is present and it's necessary to be cognizant about the present danger and personal safety. Condition Yellow is an elevated risk indicating that danger is present and that options should be considered to enhance personal safety. In this condition, there's a very brief period of time to evaluate options and take action to alleviate danger. Condition Red is when a dangerous situation is occurring, and immediate action should be taken. Below are some examples to illustrate these mental conditions.

Larry and Mac are businessmen and have traveled outside their home state to attend a conference. After business hours, Larry and Mac go out for dinner. They walk several blocks from their hotel to a restaurant that has a great reputation for steaks and seafood. The restaurant is busy, and the two must wait at least an hour before being seated. After a great meal, Larry and Mac begin their journey back to their hotel, but they make a wrong turn. Instead of walking on well-lighted streets, the two are now walking down several streets where the streetlights are dim. Larry and Mac are concerned about their present whereabouts and begin to look for an open business where they can either use a telephone to call for a taxi or obtain directions back to the hotel. The two men are now in condition green.

Larry and Mac spot a small business in the distance that appears to be open. Walking closer to the business, it appears to be a small liquor store with several men standing in front. As Larry and Mac approach the store, the young men in front stop talking with each other and literally stare at the two strangers in their neighborhood. Larry and Mac have now entered condition blue. They enter the store and ask the store clerk for directions back to their hotel. The store clerk gives them directions and cautions them to take a taxi rather than walk. The clerk advises that they must use a telephone outside to summon a taxi. Larry and Mac leave the store and use the pay phone outside the store to summon a taxi. The young men approach them and engage them in idle conversation. As Larry and Mac speak with these men, they notice the men have encircled them—two in front of them and one on each side. Larry and Mac position themselves with their backs to the outside wall of the store. They now find themselves deeply into condition blue, quickly approaching condition yellow.

Larry and Mac sense that these men are really not interested in chit chatting about current events—they are far more interested in their personal belongings. One of the men asks Larry if he has a couple of dollars to spare. When Larry says no, the man on Larry's right side says, "Hey, nice jacket." The man reaches behind him with his right hand as if to obtain a weapon. Larry and Mac can wait no longer. They are in condition red and must respond. Larry turns to the man on his right and places his right hand on the man's right arm, momentarily keeping the man from removing his right hand. As the man attempts to strike with his left hand, Larry uses a left punch to the man's torso, followed by a left elbow strike to the head, knocking the assailant out. Mac, seeing that his friend has begun to defend himself against an attack and fearing that the other assailants will attack, launches a counteroffensive. He strikes the assailant to his left with a left sidekick to the knee followed by a left palm strike to the assailant's chin. Mac then uses a right punch to the assailant's solar plexus immediately followed by a left elbow strike to the face, causing the assailant to crumple to the ground.

Larry turns slightly to his left and notices the assailant standing in front of him has begun a right hand punch at his head. Larry blocks the punch with his left hand and simultaneously strikes the assailant with a knife hand strike to his neck. Larry delivers a left punch to the assailant's body followed by a left roundhouse kick to the groin and solar plexus, causing the assailant to fall to the ground.

Meanwhile, Mac has noticed the remaining assailant has produced a broken bottle and is about to launch a backhand strike toward his head. Mac blocks the assailant's bottle-wielding strike with his right hand and places the assailant in an arm break position. Because the assailant has a weapon, Mac is forced to break the assailant's right elbow, followed by a right hand strike to the throat.

Larry and Mac have quickly and effectively defended themselves against an attack. They run back to their hotel, where they call 911 to report the incident and request an ambulance for the incapacitated assailants.

As their situation escalated rapidly from green to blue to yellow to red, Larry and Mac used their mental conditions to sense danger and to prepare mentally and physically for the upcoming altercation. If they did so, they would be far better off than someone who did not heed the conditions and panicked or acted rashly.

DANGER ERRORS

Danger errors signal problems in a person's ability to see a situation as it really is and to note the presence of danger. Recognizing and correcting these errors helps a defender develop the proper mental frame of mind during training and in the actual application of the tactics and techniques.

1. **Relaxing too soon.** When a dangerous situation presents itself, the defender must take immediate action to maximize his or her safety. The defender's actions may or may not include physical force against an assailant; the physical action may entail merely moving to a better location. After moving, however, the defender must not relax prematurely, because danger might still be present. The defender must stay watchful, aware of the surroundings and the people in the area.

2. **Tombstone courage.** A person with tombstone courage has no realistic fear of a situation. For example, when looking down a deserted dark alley, instead of recognizing the potential danger lurking there, he sees the opportunity to engage in a physical confrontation. Even worse, he does not even consider the potential of an attack taking place there. Tombstone courage provides a false sense of security and invites trouble.

3. **Preoccupation.** Someone whose mind is on other things is not the least bit aware of the environment, the people in the environment, or the potential dangers of the environment. People who are preoccupied wade deep into a situation and then wonder how and why all these problems are suddenly occurring around them.

For example, Janet gets lost while driving in a strange city, so she pulls over to the curb to look at a map. She does not observe the environment she is driving through, nor does she open up the map discreetly. Instead, she spreads the map across the windshield, concealing her view of the environment while also making it easily apparent to anyone nearby that she is unfamiliar with the area. Janet is so preoccupied with trying to find her way that she does not take the time to observe her environment. If she did, she would note the presence of the seedy-looking characters standing on the sidewalk next to her vehicle.

4. **Complacent.** Complacent people don't think about their surroundings. They are the ones who, when told that a serial killer is on the loose in their area, think that nothing terrible can happen to them or their loved ones. They venture out into places a sensible person would avoid.

Training can mentally prepare a defender to deal with any assailant. Be prepared to use whatever level of force necessary to stop the assailant—even deadly force. Train the body to respond to the physical challenges that a violent altercation may bring. If the mind or body is not prepared to meet and overcome the challenges of battle, perhaps the best course of action when facing the moment of truth may be to escape or de-escalate the situation. Having previously mentally rehearsed many times what situations will most likely take place and having considered all the options, the defender will confidently choose the best course of action.

The harsh reality of the world is that sometimes good people become victims of crime. When that fateful moment arrives, expeditiously move into the mindset you need to be victorious, implement the best plan, and don't stop until you reach the desired result.

The most important result in any attack is survival. No matter what a defender does, if he or she lives through the attack—it was the right choice! Always remember that there is no one way to avoid ever becoming a crime victim, nor is there just one tactic to stay safe. The defender may have to employ any number of mental tactics and physical techniques to successfully defeat an assailant. Self-defense must prepare the mind and body for an encounter long before any confrontation takes place. The defender must be capable of meeting and overcoming all the challenges that an assailant may initiate.

In every defensive encounter, the defender must possess the ability to "stand and deliver." Regardless of the jumble of emotions that will certainly be present, a potential victim who has made the decision to engage in self-defense must never allow emotions to inhibit his or her movements and render the defense unsuccessful.

Confidence, not a false sense of security, is a huge element in being effective. Remember that pain can be inflicted on the assailant, and counterstrikes that hit the right targets will produce the desired results. Any defender who allows fear to prevail will be unable to effectively complete any self-defense technique or tactic.

3

CONDITIONING AND BASIC MOVES

Before beginning any physical training, get the advice and approval of your physician. Most physicians are familiar with the types of movements and routines used in martial arts and self-defense training and can talk to you about restrictions and pre-existing medical conditions. Anyone entering a training program should also undergo a physical fitness evaluation to learn their individual strengths and areas for improvement. This evaluation should be administered by a professional. Most fitness gyms have trainers who can perform a fitness evaluation. Once you have established a physical fitness baseline, you will know where you may or may not need improvement.

THE WARM-UP

To prepare for any self-defense training session, the body needs to warm up. Warming up loosens the muscles and increases blood circulation. Lack of a proper warm-up before training significantly increases the potential for injury during the session and in subsequent sessions. Some people are naturally flexible and may have the false impression that they do not require a warm-up. This might work for some people in the short term, but sooner or later an injury will occur.

A proper warm-up has at least three components: stimulating blood circulation to the various muscle groups, flexibility and stretching, and strength building. Expect to spend about 5 to 10 minutes on each of these areas. Incorporate a routine of calisthenics consisting of 50 jumping jacks, which will get the blood flowing. Include a repetition of 50 push-ups and 50 sit-ups as a strength-building portion of the warm-up.

If these repetitions are initially too difficult, start with fewer repetitions and work up to these amounts. Perform the movements correctly and consistently to allow gradual improvement. In almost no time, you will not only meet the recommended beginning repetitions but will surpass them.

Other strength-building exercises may consist of weight training or isometrics. Take extreme care when incorporating weight training into a self-defense training routine. Ensure that you do not lose flexibility as a result of heavy weight training. The overall goal of strength building should not detract from other portions of training, and you should not compromise one aspect for another. Flexibility should increase, not decrease, over time.

After completing the initial warm-up routine, include a minimum of 10 minutes for a stretching routine. Be sure to focus on the major muscle groups that you will use during subsequent training. Injuries such as pulled or strained leg muscles usually occur because the muscle was not properly warmed up and is being called on to do something it is not prepared to do. Always take the time to stretch properly during this phase to reduce the potential for injuries. Start from the neck and slowly work down the body to loosen up. Using this stretching routine ensures that you cover all the areas you'll use. It takes time to properly stretch so that all muscle groups will be prepared to function during subsequent routines.

FLEXIBILITY EXERCISES

NECK

This exercise is designed to loosen the neck muscles. Stand with feet shoulder-width apart and arms at sides. Slowly rotate the head and neck in a clockwise direction, keeping the neck as relaxed as possible. Make at least four complete revolutions before changing to a counterclockwise direction. Make the same number of revolutions. This exercise should take approximately two minutes to complete.

SHOULDER ROTATION

With feet shoulder-width apart, raise both arms out from the body until they are even with the shoulders. Slowly rotate the arms in small circles in one direction, allowing the shoulder joints to do the majority of the work. Slowly increase the size of the circles until the arms overlap and cross each other. Once the arms overlap, reverse the direction of the circles and work back to the small circles. This exercise should take approximately two minutes to complete.

SITTING LEG STRETCH

Sit on the floor with both legs directly out in front of the body. This stretch is a three-part process. First, move the legs outward from the center of the body, as close as possible to a 45-degree angle. Ensure that the back side of each leg is relaxed and remains on the floor with both knees straight. Maintain this leg position for at least one minute to allow the leg muscles to get accustomed to the stretch. Next, keeping the back straight, slowly move the chin forward as if to touch the chin to the shin of one leg. Then relax and slowly move the chin to the other shin. Continue to move the legs outward as far as possible, repeating the three-part process each time. Once you achieve the maximum flexibility and distance (180 degrees) or begin to feel pain during the routine, slowly move legs back to the starting position. This stretching exercise should take at least 10 minutes to complete. If you experience intense pain while doing any leg stretch, slowly reverse the process to relieve pain. The goal is to slowly increase flexibility without causing injuries.

SITTING BUTTERFLY STRETCH

Sit on the floor and place the bottoms of your feet together with knees bent at approximately a 45-degree angle. Holding both ankles, pull the feet close to the groin area. Still holding onto both ankles, use both elbows to push both knees toward the floor. This exercise should take approximately one minute.

BACK STRETCH

Lie on your back. Place both arms, with palms down, on the floor toward the feet. Keeping feet together, lift the feet toward the head until the toes touch the floor over the top of the head. Keep the palms of both hands on the floor to maintain balance. Hold this position for approximately one minute while breathing deeply; the emphasis is on stretching the muscles in the lower back. After one minute has elapsed, slowly move both feet back to their original position.

Take a rest before beginning the technique training, but be sure that the rest period is no longer than five minutes. Any longer than that will allow the body to cool off too much and lose the benefits of the warm-up.

THE WORKOUT

Practice the individual self-defense movements. A session should include the blocks and stances found in this chapter, as well as hand strikes and kicks from chapters 4 and 6, each as individual movements. As an example, do 50 repetitions of a rising block. The quality of each move, not the number of repetitions, will produce proficiency.

After proficiency is gained with the individual components, refer to the technique chapters dealing with the defense against a punch or a kick or other self-defense movements. These chapters contain movements that combine the individual components into a series of movements that is called a "technique." An example of a technique would be to perform the following movements to defend against a right punch: left outer forearm block, right hammerfist strike to the jaw, left punch to the ribs, followed by a right hammerfist strike to the temple.

Slowly practice many repetitions for a selected technique to develop the form of the movement as well as muscle memory. Maintain the stances for the chosen technique to condition the legs. Practicing in front of a mirror can help focus on the form. After proficiency has been gained for that technique, practice the technique on the other side of the body. This is accomplished by simply reversing the technique in terms of left versus right. If the technique called for blocking with the left hand and stepping with the left foot into a stance while striking with the right hand, reverse the movements so that whatever is designated for one side is now done on the other side of the body. The technique would then consist of blocking with the right hand and stepping with the right foot into a stance while striking with the left hand. Practice the technique on this side with just as many repetitions as on the first side the technique was initially practiced. By practicing on both sides of the body, the defender will more than likely be capable of defending an attack coming from either side of the body and not just on one side. At this stage, do not add speed to any portion of the technique. It's most important to perform the movements correctly.

SELF-DEFENSE MOVEMENTS

In self-defense, how a defender stands, blocks, punches, and kicks are all integral components that make up the foundation of movement. Without the proper foundation, the defender will be incapable of performing any technique at a high level of proficiency.

BLOCKS

A *block* is an arm or leg movement designed to stop or deflect the incoming strike of an assailant. Blocks are essential to any self-defense technique, and the majority of self-defense situations will call for a defender to deploy them.

Some people think that a block alone will deter an attack. It is true that a block used in isolation will deter an attack, but only momentarily. Unless a defender inflicts significant pain on the assailant, the attack that is momentarily deterred will continue—with renewed intensity. A defender who fails to successfully block or deflect an incoming strike will not be able to employ any other element of a self-defense technique.

When you are first learning a blocking tactic, the basic method you practice may involve additional physical movements that help set up the block. For an example, when first learning to do a downward block, you move the blocking arm all the way up to the ear before actually moving down to block the incoming strike. As you gain proficiency, however, you can eliminate the movements that are nonessential to the practical application of the tactic. Never wind up before executing any block. The assailant will see the windup and exploit the move by striking the defender before the block ever makes contact with the intended target.

Numerous blocks can be used to protect the head, torso, and lower portions of the defender's body effectively. The particular block to use to divert an incoming strike depends on several factors: the angle of the incoming strike, the position of the defender, and the subsequent movements or counterstrikes that the defender intends to deploy. Observing the angle and the target area of the assailant's incoming strike will also enable the defender to block more effectively. A defender develops these observation skills by watching a variety of strikes being executed and by practicing extensively.

The aggressor might punch in either a straight line or in a circular direction. If the aggressor's punch is delivered in a straight line, any block designed to cover that area on the defender's body can be deployed. It's when the aggressor punches in a circular direction that the choice of which block to use is much more critical. Using an incorrect block against a circular direction punch fails to stop the incoming strike, causing the defender to be struck and rendered incapable of further defensive actions.

When defending against an aggressor's right circular direction punch, the defender should use the left hand to block the attack. This prevents the incoming strike from being pulled into the defender's head or body. When defending against a left circular direction punch, the defender should use the right hand to block the attack.

There are two types of blocking contacts: hard and soft. In a *hard block*, force meets force. The defender makes contact with the assailant's incoming strike in a manner that causes injury to the body part the assailant has chosen to use for the strike. For example, if the assailant has chosen to throw a punch, the defender would make contact with the wrist area of the assailant's punching arm, injuring it. If the assailant executes a kick, the defender's block would simultaneously block the kick and injure the kicking leg at the ankle. These injuries deter subsequent strikes from the assailant.

A *soft block* is a movement in which the defender makes direct contact with the assailant's attacking tool but does not injure the assailant. This type of block merely deflects the incoming strike. In a soft block, the defender typically uses the palm of the hand or the fingers to reroute the incoming strike. A block of this nature is appropriate for use by intermediate- to advanced-level self-defense practitioners. Study the photographs depicting these basic blocks; these movements will be integral to the majority of the techniques in this book.

RISING BLOCK

The rising block is a hard block designed to protect the defender's head and face. The block begins in the center of the chest and moves in a straight line to its ending position just above the head. The only portion of the body that moves when using this block are the arms. The only portions of the defender's arms that come into contact with the aggressor's punch are the wrist and lower forearm area.

This block is best suited to any attack where the strike is moving in a straight line to the head or face of the defender. Begin by placing both arms across the chest with the hands closed in a fist, palms and fingers of both hands facing the chest. The arm closest to the body will be the arm designated to perform the block. Each hand angles toward the opposite shoulder (right fist toward the left shoulder and left fist toward the right shoulder), with the elbows down and held close to the rib cage. The arms should be approximately three inches away from the chest. Perform the left rising block by moving the left arm up until the left wrist is directly in front of the face, then rotate the arm outward until the inside and most fleshy portion of the left arm is facing the direction of the incoming attack.

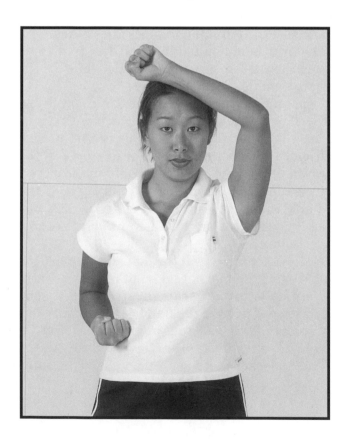

At this point, the left arm is bent at a slight angle, with the hand slightly higher than the elbow. As the left arm moves upward to deploy a left rising block, the right hand, still in a closed fist, simultaneously moves down from the position near the chest to rest against the right hip with the palm area facing upward. This position of the right hand is called the recoil position. When practicing this block without an incoming strike, rotate the blocking arm over prior to the final position of the block. For a rising block to be done with the right hand, simply reverse the instructions for left hand to right hand.

To understand the blocking surfaces of a left rising block, place the left hand palm down on a table. As the defender's block makes contact with the incoming strike, the initial area of contact is on the wrist and lower forearm closest to the thumb, then the back of the wrist, and finally the side of the wrist closest to the little finger.

By rotating the wrist of the blocking arm while blocking the incoming punch, the force of the incoming strike is equally dispersed among all three areas of the blocking left arm, and the left arm will not have to absorb the impact of a punch in just one area.

FOREARM BLOCK

The forearm block is a hard block also designed to protect the defender's head and face. The block begins at one side of the body and moves in a straight line across the defender's body to its ending position on the opposite side. Both the upper body and arms move when using this block. The only portion that contacts the aggressor's punching arm is the inside and fleshy portion of the wrist and outer forearm area of the defender's blocking arm.

This block can be deployed against a punch to the face moving in a straight line or in a circular direction. In the same way as the rising block, if the aggressor is striking with a right straight-line punch, the

defender may use either the right or left forearm block. However, if the aggressor is executing a right-hand punch in a circular direction, the defender must use a right forearm block to block the punch.

Begin the right forearm block by closing the right hand in a fist and placing it next to the right ear with the fingers of the inside portion of the right hand facing out. Position the left arm horizontally across the chest, with the left hand closed (palm downward) directly in front of the right pectoral muscle. Move the right hand from its initial position toward the front of the body while simultaneously moving the left hand to the recoil position (refer to the rising block instructions). In the ending position for this block, the right hand is directly in front of the left pectoral muscle, and the right elbow is in the center of the body. The blocking arm also rotates so the inside portion of the right arm faces the body. The blocking surface begins with the inner most fleshy portion of the right wrist and lower forearm, and as the wrist rotates, the outer portion of the right wrist is brought into contact. As with the rising block, the rotation of the blocking wrist redirects the incoming strike and disperses the energy of the punch across the blocking wrist area.

OUTER FOREARM BLOCK

The outer forearm block is a hard block also designed to protect the defender's head and face area. The block begins in the center of the chest and moves in a straight line to its ending position. The only part of the body that moves when using this block is the arms. The only portions of the defender's arms that will contact the aggressor's punch are the wrist and lower forearm.

This block can be deployed against a punch to the face moving in a straight line or in a circular direction. If the aggressor is striking with a right straight-line punch, the defender may use either the right or left outer forearm block. However, if the aggressor is executing a right hand punch in a circular direction, the defender must use a left outer forearm block to effectively block the punch.

Begin by placing both arms across the chest with the hands closed in fists, palms and fingers of both hands facing the chest. The arm closest to the body will be the arm designated to perform the block. Each hand angles toward the opposite shoulder (right fist toward the left shoulder and left fist toward the right shoulder) with elbows down and held close to the rib cage. The arms should be about three inches from the chest.

Deploy the left block by moving the left arm away from the chest area out toward the left side of the body. The left arm will rotate, exposing the inside portion of the left forearm toward the aggressor. The blocking surface begins with the inside portion of the left wrist and lower forearm and as the wrist rotates, the outer portion of the left wrist is brought into contact. As with the rising block and forearm blocks, the rotation of the blocking wrist redirects the incoming strike and disperses the energy of the punch across the blocking wrist area.

PALM BLOCK

Although a variety of other soft blocks exist, the palm block is the only soft block used in this book. The palm block allows the same blocking action as the forearm block, however the blocking surface is the fleshy portion of the hand. A block of this type is specifically designed not to make "hard" contact with a strike but merely to deflect the incoming strike and facilitate a quicker response. This block is best suited to any attack where the strike is moving in a straight line to the head or face of the defender. The disadvantage of this block is that it cannot be used against a punch delivered in a circular direction. As

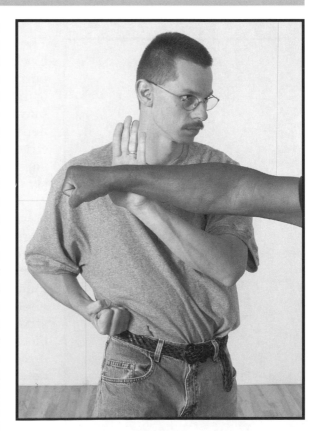

an example, if the defender attempted to use a left palm block against an aggressor who is punching with a right punch, the defender would more than likely move the incoming punch too close into their body. Attempting to use a left block against a right circular direction punch, the aggressor will have too much power in the punch and the strength of the punch will overwhelm the block.

This block is simple yet complex. Move the blocking hand to meet the straight-line punch and make contact with the palm to deflect the punch away from the body. When the assailant uses a right straight-line punch, the defender may use either a right or left palm block. The incoming strike will be deflected in a sideways movement away from the defender. The complexity of this block is that the contact is made only with the palm of the blocking hand as the blocking surface. In comparison, the other blocks used the wrist and lower forearm area, which provides more of a surface area to make contact with the incoming strike. The defender must be very accurate when using this block because of the smaller blocking surface.

DOWNWARD BLOCK

The downward block is a hard block designed to protect the lower portion of the body against a punch or a kick. This block can be deployed against a punch or kick delivered in a straight line or in a circular direction. If the aggressor is striking with a right straight-line punch, the defender may use either the right or left downward block. However, if the aggressor is executing a right-hand punch or right kick in a circular direction, the defender must use a left downward block to effectively block the incoming strike. If the defender attempts to block an assailant's right circular direction punch or kick with the defender's right downward block, the incoming strike would be placed too close into the defender's body possibly even striking the defender.

Begin by closing both hands in a fist. Place the right fist against the front of the left hip area with the palm and fingers facing the body. Place the left fist near the right shoulder with the fleshy portion of the left hand lightly touching the right shoulder. The elbows of both arms rest gently against the front of the body.

Perform a left downward block by moving the left hand down the right arm towards the left hip area, rotating the left hand upon contact of the incoming strike so that the left hand will end with the left closed hand outside the left thigh. The right hand still in a closed fist will simultaneously move upward from the position near the left thigh to rest against the right hip with the palm area facing upward.

The left blocking arm will have the elbow slightly bent to absorb the shock from the contact of the incoming strike. The blocking surface on the defender's blocking arm is the entire outer edge of the arm.

WRIST BLOCK

The wrist block is a hard block designed to protect the lower portion of the body against a punch or kick. Unlike the downward block, which uses the outside of the wrist as a contact surface for the block, the wrist block uses the inside of the wrist as the blocking surface. The wrist block works best when the assailant deploys a straight-line strike with the hand or foot.

Close the left hand into a fist and extend the left arm down so that the left fist is directly in front of the left thigh. Deploy the block by simply moving the left arm across to the right thigh in a straight line. In this block the left arm will travel only about 12 inches. The blocking surface for the wrist block extends about 6 inches along the inside of the wrist.

X BLOCK

The X block is a hard block designed to block either the head, the face, or lower torso. This block allows both hands to make contact with the incoming strike at exactly the same time, allowing the defender to execute the first counterstrike while momentarily keeping one hand on the incoming strike.

To execute an X block that protects the head and face, simply form an X with both arms extended just above the head with the inner, most fleshy portions of the forearms facing toward the aggressor. The hands should be about four inches apart, which is sufficient to capture the incoming strike between both hands. It's immaterial whether the left hand is closest or furthest from the aggressor as the block is executed.

The position of the elbows is about 14 inches apart. Both arms will touch about 2 inches above the head. The contact area of this block is

between both hands as the arms form an X, which exposes the outer portion of both the left and right wrist areas.

To execute an X block to protect the lower torso, form an X with both arms extended just below the waist with the inner, most fleshy portions of the forearms facing the defender. The hands should be about four inches apart, which is sufficient to capture the incoming strike between both hands. It doesn't matter whether the left hand is closest or farthest from the aggressor as the block is executed. The elbows in this position are about 14 inches apart. The blocking surface is exactly the same as when defending the head area.

COUNTERSTRIKES

Counterstrikes are mandatory for self-defense. Real-life physical assailants are never deterred by mere evasive movements or just a defender blocking their strikes. If a counterstrike is not immediate and effective, the assailant will simply continue to strike until achieving the objective of overcoming the defender and rendering him or her helpless. Place counterstrikes where the assailant is not expecting them and in an area that will have devastating effects. Study the techniques in this book to learn exactly where to execute those counterstrikes for the most successful defense.

Certain target areas of the assailant's body are more desirable than others for the defender to strike. Other areas are best avoided. For example, punching to the head or face is almost a natural reaction for most people involved in a fight. But the head is the hardest surface area of the body, and a defender who executes the strike improperly is very likely to fracture the hand. Also, a defender should never punch an assailant in the mouth. Such a strike could result in teeth embedded in the defender's fist and a risk of subsequent infection.

The assailant's torso is a much more effective target, because it contains a substantial number of vital organs; striking these areas will cause the assailant a great deal of pain. In addition, the torso provides a softer surface for a defender's strikes.

A single kick to the groin is also overrated as a counterattack. Only rarely will one kick to the groin end a fight. For such a kick to have the best results, it should be a part of a technique that includes a variety of other movements that strike multiple target areas of the body. The totality of the defender's counterstrikes hitting multiple target areas on the assailant's body will cause the assailant to stop attacking. To maximize the effect of a kick to the groin, deliver the kick at an upward angle from between the legs and moving up.

Kicking directly to the assailant's head while he or she is standing upright is not practical. For any kick to reach the head, a hard, small target to strike, the defender must pass up numerous targets—such as the knees, groin, bladder, rib cage, and solar plexus—to which a kick could deliver a more devastating blow. The unfortunate result of an ineffective kick to the head may be that the assailant subsequently blocks the target areas the defender previously passed up. This is not to say that a kick to the head is never effective—it's just not always the best choice.

The delivery angle of a counterstrike is also an important consideration. A direct strike is delivered in a straight line between the assailant and the defender. An indirect strike reaches the intended target in a circular motion.

KIAI!

A kiai (pronounced *key-eye*) is a loud sound a person makes by exhaling air at one focused point. A kiai has several purposes in self-defense: the focus of strength of one particular strike, to tense certain muscle groups so that if the defender is struck it will have minimal physical effect over their body, to psychologically break the assailant's concentration, and to call attention to a situation. The sound of a kiai comes deep from within the diaphragm and should be loud enough to achieve all of the above purposes. The kiai sound might be as short as one second or as long as two to three seconds.

In observing other sports, a focused sound a professional athlete might make is a kiai. As an example, when a football player is anticipating contact being made with another player, a focused sound can sometimes be heard by the football player. When observing power lifters, they will often make a similar audible sound as they are lifting the weight.

In the application of a self-defense technique, a kiai is optional. Some defenders feel that it gives them more focused strength on a particular strike. By using a kiai, the aggressor may be momentarily distracted and stunned, allowing the defender to use that distraction to his or her advantage. Lastly, by using a kiai in a self-defense technique, people who were unaware that a physical altercation was or is taking place will be alerted that a dangerous situation is taking place.

STANCES

A stance is simply the position in which a defender stands while executing a block or strike. The defender will nearly always begin in a "street-ready position." When the aggressor begins his or her attack, the defender usually blocks the incoming strike. The defender may then strike the aggressor with a counterstrike or move to a position where the counterstrikes are executed. By employing the proper stance during a defensive technique, the defender can maximize power. The stances also enable the defender to stay upright in a position of safety while delivering effective counterstrikes. A stance will never be held for any longer than just a few seconds, just enough to complete the intended counterstrikes.

During an actual altercation, a defender should never assume a stance in anticipation of becoming involved in a physical altercation. Using a stance prematurely telegraphs the potential ability that a defender might have and allows the aggressor to escalate his or her intended level of violence.

Practice stances in various environments. Altercations can take place on any surface—asphalt, rough terrain such as a rocky surface, uneven surfaces such as grass or dirt, smooth surfaces such as a tile floor or polished concrete, or slippery surfaces such as icy ground or a skating rink. Take care to avoid injuries on any of these surfaces. The basic stances illustrated in this book are designed to optimize each specific technique.

STREET-READY STANCE

The street-ready stance is the position in which the defender stands before defending himself or herself in an attack situation. This position should allow the body to remain alert yet relaxed enough to begin a self-defense technique. Whenever an aggressor approaches, the defender should be poised in such a manner that reflects a nonthreatening demeanor. Standing in any other manner may signal to the aggressor that the defender is not only expecting a physical confrontation but might initiate an attack of his or her own. Plus, standing in a fight-ready manner takes away the defender's element of surprise.

In the street-ready stance, the defender stands with feet about 12 inches apart and weight distributed equally between them. Both knees are naturally and slightly bent to enable the defender to move in any direction to execute a defensive movement without first having to bend a knee. Hold the upper body in an upright position, and relax as much as possible. Hands are in front of the body. The hand closest to the body is in a closed fist, and the other hand (closest to the aggressor) protects the closed fist.

FRONT STANCE

A front stance allows the defender to withstand forward pressure or to deliver power strikes to the front. In this stance, the defender has one foot further forward than the other, with the forward knee bent and the back knee straight.

To facilitate learning, this stance will be taught moving forward with the left foot to assume a left front stance. For the defender to assume a right front stance, simply reverse the directions from left to right and vice versa. It is necessary to understand angle degrees to assist with this stance. The angle directly to the left will be ninety degrees. The angle directly ahead is designated as 0. The angle degree between the left (90 degrees) and straight ahead (0 degrees) will be designated as 45 degrees.

Begin by standing facing straight ahead with feet about 12 inches apart. Step forward with the left foot about 30 inches toward the above-described 45-degree angle. The position of the inside portion of the left foot is facing straight ahead. The left knee is bent. The position of the left leg from the ankle to the knee is in a straight vertical line. The position of the left leg from the knee to the hip is at a 45-degree angle. The back knee is locked straight. The toes of the back foot will face as straight ahead as possible. In this stance, about 60 percent of the weight is on the front foot. Hold the upper body upright.

HORSE STANCE

A horse stance allows the defender to withstand side-to-side pressure or to deliver power to the side. Begin by standing facing straight ahead with feet about 12 inches apart. Move one foot directly to the side until the distance between the feet is about 36 inches. The body weight distribution is evenly balanced on both feet.

The inside position of both feet is facing straight ahead, the same direction the chest is facing. Bend knees to lower the height about 12 inches, pushing knees slightly outward. Hold the upper body in an upright, relaxed position.

Although this stance is depicted facing straight ahead, the defender never stands facing an aggressor in this fashion. Facing the aggressor in this position allows access to too many vulnerable positions. During the actual application of this stance, the defender places the aggressor either to the left or right side by about 90 degrees.

SELF-DEFENSE TIP

Never assume any type of stance or fighting pose before an actual altercation. Assuming a stance gives the assailant advance warning that you are ready for the attack and know something about defensive tactics. The assailant may use that warning to escalate the level of violence; for example, instead of launching a fistfight, the assailant may introduce a knife or a gun.

PRACTICE WHAT YOU'VE LEARNED

Practice the individual self-defense movements you have learned. Your practice sessions should include the blocks and stances from this chapter and the hand strikes and kicks you will learn in subsequent chapters, all as individual components. As an example, practice the rising block using 50 repetitions. As stated earlier, *it is not the number of repetitions, but rather the quality of each move that will produce proficiency.*

Maintain a horse or front stance while practicing the blocks, strikes, and kicks to condition the legs and develop muscle memory. Practice in front of a mirror to pay particular attention to not only the feel of the block, but also the form of the movement. Once you have developed proficiency for the block, then practice a strike, then a kick.

Practice each move slowly to facilitate the form, the fluidity of the moves, and muscle memory. At this stage, do not add speed to any portion of the technique. It is more important to be capable of performing the movements slowly, carefully, and correctly than to perform the movements rapidly but incorrectly.

REAL-LIFE SELF-DEFENSE

Real-life assailants will stand in such a way as to disguise their offensive movements. An assailant will attempt to hide a strike by subterfuge and distraction. Some self-defense systems fail to account for the assailant's natural tendencies in real time; with the phrase "block and strike," the "and" portion of that phrase denotes a pause in the action. That pause allows the assailant to make another strike. In real time, because of the pause, the assailant has launched at least two strikes that the defender will have to answer.

The advanced practitioner of self-defense will perform the block and the first strike almost simultaneously. This involves blocking the incoming strike and immediately striking the assailant. The instant that the defender feels the contact of the block, the assailant should feel the first of several counterstrikes. Once an assailant has begun the attack, the only thing that will physiologically stop further acts of aggression is immediate pain that overcomes his or her ability to attack.

During the practice session, the proficient practitioner of self-defense should be capable of defending against the incoming strike at full speed, using proper timing to block the incoming strike yet exercising maximum control while delivering counterstrikes so as to not injure his or her practice partner. This practitioner should be fully capable of performing a spontaneous technique to counter any strike that the practice partner can execute. The defender will not know what type of strike will be executed or what target area of the body the practice partner is intending to strike. Generally, it takes several years of focused training to achieve this level of advanced proficiency.

Advanced practitioners will practice three to four techniques during an average training session. Instead of always practicing a defense for a right-hand attack to the defender's head, vary the incoming strike to include a left punch to the head area as well as strikes with either hand to the torso. The attack may not always be a right-hand punch to the head. The attack could start with a left front kick to the groin followed by a right-hand punch to the defender's body. Train to proficiently block any incoming strike to all areas, regardless of whether the attack is by hand or by foot or executed from the left or right side. The goal is to be competent in defending against a full-speed, unrehearsed, spontaneous attack from either hand or foot.

METHODOLOGY OF PHYSICAL TACTICS

The techniques in this section allow the defender to use the assailant's own body mechanics against him or her when applying a defensive technique. Each strike the defender executes sets up the following strikes. For example, a counterstrike delivered to the assailant's lower torso will force the assailant's head to move forward, closer to the defender.

The next counterstrike, delivered to the assailant's head, will make the assailant's lower torso move forward and closer to the defender. Because the aggressors' body is being manipulated in this fashion, each subsequent counterstrike will reach the desired target area much quicker than if the aggressor was standing fully erect. Another benefit of the aggressor's involuntary movement is that the impact of following counterstrikes is much greater and more effective than if the aggressor's body were standing erect and stationary at each moment of impact.

POSITIONING OF THE ASSAILANT

Each block is designed to move the assailant's punch and body into a specific predetermined position. For example, when an assailant strikes with a right straight punch to the defender's head, and the defender blocks with a left outer forearm block, the blocking angle will open up the assailant, placing the assailant directly in front of the defender, facilitating counterstrikes to the front of the assailant's body. If the assailant were to strike with the same right straight punch to the defender's head, but this time the defender blocks with a right outer forearm block, the blocking angle will close up the assailant, placing him in such a position where his body is crossed up, and the defender is capable of delivering counterstrikes to the right side of the assailant's body. Employing a block that crosses up the assailant has an additional benefit of making it more difficult for the assailant to deliver another hand strike without needing first to change his position to turn and face the defender.

Each of these positions offers advantages and disadvantages. The advantage of opening up the assailant is that you can deliver counterstrikes directly to the front of the assailant's body. The disadvantage of this positioning is that the assailant can strike back with either hand because the defender is directly in front of the assailant.

The advantages of closing up the assailant and striking the lateral and posterior side of the assailant is that he or she will have to make a major turning movement to locate the defender before attempting any additional strikes. Another advantage is that the defender is not standing directly in front of the assailant making themselves susceptible to the assailant's powerful strikes. The disadvantage is that the defender is not in a position to strike to the anterior (front) areas of the assailant's body; however, the lateral and posterior (side and rear) areas are easily within reach.

Once you have become competent at closing off the assailant's subsequent strikes, you can easily employ the principle of lateral movement. When performing techniques involving lateral movement, the defender is literally capable of moving behind the assailant to deliver counterstrikes.

In some self-defense systems, the assailant moves in a straight line towards the defender. When the defender moves to a position to deliver counterstrikes, the defender steps backward in the same straight line the assailant was attacking on.

When employing lateral movement, the defender does not step backward on the same straight attacking line, but moves off at a lateral angle. This movement allows the attacker to stay on the straight line, but allows the defender to move off the line. By moving off the line and keeping the assailant on line, the defender is capable of delivering effective counterstrikes to the extremely vulnerable side and rear of the assailant. Lateral movements will be illustrated further in chapter 5.

Once having gained proficiency in self-defense techniques, the defender must maintain that level of competency. The elements of timing, speed, accuracy, and proper tactics have a significant effect on physical technique. If you do not practice and improve on these elements, it is very likely that when you need to use these tactics and techniques, they will not bring the desired results.

PHYSICAL SIGNS OF AN ATTACK

Untrained people are incapable of executing a power punch without providing physical clues as they deliver the strike. Though executing the punch at full speed, the assailant will exhibit most if not all of the common clues during the strike. The ability to observe these physical clues requires a keen sense for movement.

For each power punch executed, the untrained or unsophisticated assailant will involuntarily telegraph the type of punch he or she is going to throw as well as its intended target. Signs that a power punch is on its way include but are not limited to the following:

- The assailant has encroached into the defender's critical distance.
- The assailant's facial expression changes to reflect his or her intensity.
- The assailant's intended striking hand is clenched into a fist.
- The assailant's body is turned slightly sideways, with the intended striking hand farther away from the defender. (This will give the assailant's punch maximum power.)
- The assailant shifts weight onto the forward foot, toward the defender.
- The assailant raises one or both hands like a boxer.
- The assailant's shoulders begin to rotate to allow the power punch to move forward toward the intended target.
- The assailant's striking hand begins traveling toward the intended target.

An assailant planning to initiate a power kick will also provide some involuntary clues as to the type of kick being executed as well as the intended target. Signs that a power kick is coming include but are not limited to the following:

1. The assailant has encroached into the defender's critical distance.
2. The assailant's facial expression changes to reflect his or her intensity.
3. The assailant shifts weight onto the supporting leg.
4. The knee of the kicking leg lifts, providing some clue as to the kick to be executed.
   - If the assailant's knee is lifted to the front, expect a front kick.
   - If the assailant's knee is lifted to the side with the kicking foot in a somewhat horizontal line with the knee and leg, expect a roundhouse kick.
   - If the assailant is facing away by 90 degrees and the kicking knee is lifted, expect a side kick or a roundhouse kick.
   - If the assailant is facing away by 180 degrees with the kicking leg lifted, expect a back kick.
5. The assailant's striking foot will begin traveling toward the intended target. This movement will distinctly indicate the kick being executed.

Understanding the principles of weight distribution will enable the defender to know the kick an assailant is capable of executing. As an example, an assailant who places the majority of their body weight on one leg immediately renders that leg incapable of delivering a kick. Any immediate kicking threat would come from the opposite leg. To kick with the weight-bearing leg, the assailant would have to shift weight onto the other leg and then execute a kick. If the assailant is standing with the feet wide apart, this weight transfer is very easy to see. If the assailant is standing with the feet very close together, however, the weight transfer is very difficult to see. In this narrow stance the assailant can kick with either leg and somewhat hide the movement that a wider stance would easily reveal.

These initial signs of aggression give the defender some advance notice that an attack is underway. In spite of the warning, however, the defender will not have time to debate a variety of options but must immediately respond by implementing an appropriate course of action to enhance personal safety. This action consists of employing an appropriate block and executing defensive strikes to incapacitate the assailant.

4

HAND STRIKES

Counterstrikes are an essential part of a complete self-defense skill repertoire. These strikes must effectively discourage assailants from further attack. Someone who does not understand how to use the hands to fend off an attacker and has no specific training in these skills will respond ineffectively, with little force or accuracy. Few serious assailants will allow a potential victim the time to wind up and throw a punch, and even if they did, it is unlikely that such a blow would find its mark before the target moved.

This chapter presents several of the best hand strikes, each designed to deliver maximum force quickly to a vulnerable target area. Such defensive techniques require correct mechanics. To achieve the desired effect, the body must be in proper alignment to facilitate the hip rotation needed to execute each strike. Unless otherwise stated or shown in the technique photographs, each time a hand strike extends outward, the nonstriking hand must return to a ready position. When striking, always allow the elbows of the punching arm to remain slightly bent to absorb the shock of the strike. Otherwise, hyperextension of the elbow joint could occur.

Counterstrikes are meant to inflict a varying degree of pain on the aggressor, ranging from moderate discomfort to serious pain or even death. Study each of the maneuvers carefully and commit the vulnerable target areas to memory. Although one counterstrike is not likely to ward off most adept assailants, a single well-placed strike can stun an attacker to the point where the defender can either flee to a safe location or gain sufficient time to employ another self-defense technique.

Learn to punch equally with the left and right hands. Most people are right-handed and comfortable using only the right hand to deliver strikes. However, using only the dominant hand affords the defender only

25 percent of his or her potential striking tools. That is, of a potential four available weapons (two hands and two feet), he or she uses only one hand. Using both left and right hands increases the potential striking tools from 25 to 50 percent. Becoming ambidextrous in punching requires conscious repetitions with both hands.

As with any new movement, gaining proficiency requires considerable time and patience. Practice the movement slowly at first, emphasizing correctness of form. Concentrated effort over a significant length of time will result in mastery of the overall movement and equal dexterity on both sides of the body. Only then should speed and power be added to the punch.

Other important factors for the strike include focus (accurate delivery of the strike to the intended target) and control over the movement. For our purposes, *control* can be defined as the ability to know exactly how hard and how close to deliver a particular strike. Using control when practicing a technique means that the strike will not actually hit the target but come within a fraction of the target. Using control when involved in an actual altercation involves the defender striking the target with the intended power.

Ideal target areas for punches are almost unlimited. Beginning self-defense practitioners should be aware, however, that a punch delivered to the assailant's head will make contact with the hardest contact surface of the body. The head is a hard target, and proper punch position is imperative to avoid injury to the hand. Proper punch position will be discussed later in this chapter. Other target areas such as those in the torso (e.g., solar plexus, rib cage, liver, kidney) are softer and not as apt to injure the defender's hand during the delivery of a counterstrike.

Although strikes to all parts of the body, when used in an effective combination, can potentially incapacitate an assailant, certain areas offer the greatest amount of stopping power. Punches delivered to the assailant's temple, neck, throat, sternum, solar plexus, rib cage, bladder, and groin offer a greater likelihood of success.

HAND STRIKE DISTANCES

The defender will always need to account for the distance he or she will use when delivering counterstrikes. There are basically two distinct distances: (1) one where the full range of an intended hand strike reaches the target and (2) one where only half of the range of intended hand strikes reach the target.

The easiest way to visualize the difference between the two distances is to extend your punching arm to its full extension. The area around the closed fist is the full-range, and the area around the elbow is the half-range. These distances are important when using hand strikes to counter the assailant's attack. With one exception, all the punches described in this book should be delivered at their maximum extended distance. The exception is the elbow strike, which is delivered at the half-range distance.

The defender should not overextend any strike. Overextending refers to reaching far beyond the intended distance of a particular strike. Overextending a strike decreases the strike's power and might make the defender lose balance.

Defenders should always deliver counterstrikes at their maximum effective distance. Allowing each hand to be extended to its full and intended distance avoids crowding the strike. Crowding a hand strike diminishes power and allows an assailant to get too close to the defender during a counterattack.

DEVELOPING PUNCHING POWER

No windup is used to deliver hand strikes. The movement of the hips and shoulders generates the power that each of these strikes requires. To develop punching power, first be sure to use the proper mechanics when executing any punch. The punch must employ the hips, not just the arm. Proper use of the hips generates much more power in the punch. As the speed of the punch increases, the power of the punch will naturally increase as well.

Lock the wrist in the proper position. This position is slightly different for each hand strike. For all strikes that employ the knuckles when punching, the wrist should be locked in as follows. Raise the punching arm to shoulder level with the palm side of the hand facing the ground; make a fist. Look down and over the top of the punching arm to align the wrist. Move the punching hand slightly to the outside so that the knuckles of the index finger and middle finger are directly in line with the forearm of the punching arm.

For all strikes that involve the fleshy part of the hand, the wrist position is as follows. Close both fists and place them on a table with fingers facing each other. Slightly rotate each hand, forearm, and elbow so that the fleshy portion of each hand is the only part touching the table. This is the position you use to deliver the knife hand and hammer fist strikes.

If the wrist is not locked into the proper position at the moment of impact, it can be forced into a position that can cause a fracture. A strong wrist position also affects the amount of power each punch delivers. This is why boxers use wrist wraps to secure their wrists in proper alignment and prevent injuries. Although these wraps could be used in training, wearing wrist straps does not mean you are not responsible for learning proper wrist position. During real-life altercations, you won't have time to put on wrist straps before defending yourself!

Each hand strike involving contact with the knuckles will slightly rotate from its start position. This rotation allows for even more power to be delivered. The rotation occurs just as the strike is beginning to touch the intended target and completes as the strike moves deeper into the target. Rotating the hand before making contact with a target does not increase power. Think of screwing in a screw with a screwdriver. You begin turning the screwdriver once you have the screwdriver inside the screw, not before.

Although other hand strikes exist, the ones described in this chapter are essential to self-defense. The front punch emphasizes moving both hands simultaneously, with each hand doing something different. When competency is gained on the front punch, the timing used when executing several front punches is similar to using hand strike combinations (described later in this chapter and in other chapters). The remaining hand strikes are recommended in the techniques outlined in this book.

FRONT PUNCH

Begin by assuming a horse stance (see chapter 3). Close each hand into a fist, with the thumb on the outside, and extend the left arm out straight so the left fist is directly out in front and at the center of the body at face level, palm facing down.

Place the right arm against the right side of the body, wrist resting gently against the hip and palm facing up. To generate the next punch, both hands move at exactly the same time; the left hand retracts to the left hip as the right arm extends until the right fist is in the punch position. Just as the hands reach their final positions, both hands simultaneously rotate over. The final position for the right-hand punch will have the right hand extended to a punch position with palm facing down; the left hand will be against the left hip with palm facing up. To execute the next punch, simply move both hands at the same time, placing the left hand in front in a punch position and retracting the right hand to the right hip area. Just as both hands reach their final position, rotate both hands over so that the striking hand has the punch extended and palm side facing up.

Always keep the elbow of the punching arm slightly bent to absorb any shock from impact. Throughout the punch delivery and rotation, keep shoulders square. This applies to both the left and right punch.

In this punching position, the only part of the fist that will make contact with the intended target are the knuckles of the index and middle fingers. These knuckles are usually the largest on the hand and are in direct alignment with the wrist and arm during correct execution of the punch. No other part of the fist should ever make contact in the delivery of a punch.

At first, learn this punch slowly and deliberately, emphasizing form. The punch contact surface will be the first two knuckles (index and middle fingers). After this punch is practiced and speed can be added, a natural hip movement will develop as proficiency is gained.

PALM HEEL

Perform this strike in much the same manner as the front punch, except with the bottom of the palm as the striking surface. Begin by assuming a horse stance. Place the left hand in the palm heel position, extending the left arm out straight so that the left hand is directly out in front and at the center of the body at face level, with the palm open toward the assailant. The right  hand is closed in a fist and placed against the right side of the body with the wrist resting gently against the hip, palm facing up.

To generate the next palm heel strike, both hands move at exactly the same time, the left hand retracting to the left hip as the right arm extends toward the aggressor. Just as both hands reach their final positions, hands rotate over, with the striking hand opening to expose the heel of the palm and the retracting hand closing to a fist. The final position for the right hand palm heel strike will have the right hand extended to a palm heel position with palm side facing the aggressor; the left hand will be against the left hip with palm facing up. To execute the next palm heel strike, simply move both hands at the same time, moving the left hand toward the aggressor and retracting the right hand to the right hip area. Just as both hands reach their final position, rotate both hands over so that the striking hand opens to expose the left heel of the palm and the retracting right hand is resting against the hip with the palm side facing up.

The elbow of the striking arm is bent approximately 45 degrees to expose the striking portion of the palm and absorb any shock from impact. The only part of the hand that comes into contact with the intended target is the bottom of the palm. The fingers of the striking hand are pulled back to expose the palm. No other part of the hand should make contact.

SNAP PUNCH

The snap punch is delivered from a horse stance. Draw an imaginary line from the right foot through the left foot and extending in that same direction to the left about 12 inches. This is the direction in which the punch will be delivered. The left hand will be in a fist about 12 inches from the opponent and no higher than the left shoulder; the left elbow is down to protect the rib cage. The right hand is in a closed fist and gently resting against the body. This position is called "fighting guard." In this position, the left side is closest to the aggressor. The hand designated for this punch is the right hand, which in this stance is farthest from the aggressor. To assume a fighting guard on the right side, simply reverse the instructions above.

The snap punch will always be delivered with the hand farthest from the aggressor, which provides maximum hip rotation to optimize the power of this strike.

Extend a right punch in a straight line toward the assailant's torso by punching underneath the left arm, which stays in the guard position. Punching underneath the arm allows the defender to strike without giving away the next intended movement. This position also allows the left hand to either block any incoming strike or deploy subsequent strikes.

At the moment the strike reaches its target, lean slightly over the front (left) foot and rise up onto the ball of the right foot. Once the right punching hand reaches the assailant, the punch presses approximately two inches into the target. Quickly retract the punching hand and resume the fighting guard position. The hip rotation in this punch would be the same as used by a baseball player swinging a bat. The movements of the quick extension and retraction is where the punch gets its name. A snap punch can make contact in one of two ways: the fist can be in either a vertical or a horizontal position as it strikes the target. Choose whichever position you prefer.

HAMMER FIST STRIKE

In a hammer fist strike, the fleshy portion of a closed fist nearest the pinky finger strikes the target area. A defender can use a hammer fist strike in either a downward angle or in a reverse angle. A downward angle would be the same angle as one would use when using a hammer to drive a nail straight down into a surface. For the ease of explanation, only one side will be used to illustrate this strike. In order to strike with the opposite side, simply reverse the directions from one side to the other, left to right and vice versa. Assume a front stance (see chapter 3) with the left foot forward. Place the right hand in a closed fist directly adjacent to the right ear with the right elbow up and extending out to the right side. Move the right hand in a downward angle from the ear toward the intended target. The striking action is the same as if a hammer were in the right hand. Target areas for this strike angle are the head and upper torso.

A reverse angle hammer fist strike would be the same as one would use when using a backhand stroke in tennis. Assume a front stance with the left foot forward. Place the right hand in a closed fist and lay it on top of the left shoulder with the right elbow lightly resting against the chest. Move the right hand in a reverse angle toward the intended target. The striking action is the same as if using a backhand stroke in tennis with the tennis racket in the right hand. Target areas for this strike angle are the head and lower torso.

KNIFE HAND STRIKE

A knife hand strike is an open-hand strike. The fleshy part of the hand nearest the pinky finger strikes the target. A defender can use a knife hand strike in the same angles as the hammer fist strikes, (downward angle or reverse angle).

Assume a front stance (see chapter 3) with the left foot forward. Open the right hand with fingers extended and together with fingertips pointing to the right ear and the right elbow up and extending out to the right side. Move the right hand in a downward angle from the ear toward the intended target. The striking action is the same as if a hammer were in the right hand. Target areas for this strike angle are the head, neck, throat and upper torso. For the strike to reach into the neck or throat, the strike will rotate to palm up position.

A reverse angle knife hand strike is the position used for a backhand stroke in tennis. Assume a front stance with the left foot forward. Open the right hand with fingers extended and together. Place the right palm on top of the left shoulder with right elbow lightly resting against the chest. Move the right hand in a reverse angle toward the intended target. The striking action is the same as a backhand stroke in tennis with the racket in the right hand. Target areas for this strike angle are the head, neck, rib cage, and groin. For ease of explanation, only one side was used to illustrate this strike. To strike with the opposite side, reverse directions from left to right and vice versa.

ELBOW STRIKE

The elbow is a devastating weapon and one of the most underused tools in the self-defense hand strike arsenal. The elbow carries with it the power of the entire shoulder and body.

Execution of the elbow strike is similar to that of the snap punch. Begin this strike by assuming a horse stance with the fighting guard (as

described for the snap punch) toward the left side. The elbow strike will be executed with the hand furthest away from the aggressor in the same manner as a snap punch. Instead of delivering the striking right hand to the target, however, place it next to the chest so the right elbow extends toward the aggressor.

At the moment the strike reaches its intended target, lean slightly over the front (left) foot which will cause the rear (right) foot to move from its previously fully seated position, in a horse stance, onto the ball of the foot. As the elbow makes contact with the intended target, press approximately two inches into the target. Retract the striking elbow just as quickly as it extended and resume the left fighting guard position. The hip rotation in this punch is the same rotation used by a baseball player when swinging a baseball bat. Potential target areas include the head and torso.

Hand Combinations

Seldom will a single strike be sufficient to either deter an assailant or overcome an actual physical attack. For that reason, after mastering the individual hand strikes and kicks, a defender must learn to use them in combination. These combinations require the elements of replacement theory and contraction and expansion theory.

Replacement Theory

Replacement theory refers to the timing of the defender's hand strikes. Once the defender completes a strike and moves the hand away from the target, the next strike must immediately strike another target, replacing the one just finished so as not to allow any gap between strikes. Any significant gap may allow the assailant time to escape or counter the defender.

A simple drill can help explain this theory. Jane places her right hand palm down on a designated spot on a table. Jack stands ready to quickly place his hand on the spot when Jane moves her hand away.

Jane moves her right hand off the designated spot, but before Jack has a chance to move his hand in, she quickly replaces it with her left hand. When she moves her left hand off the spot, she immediately replaces it with her right hand again. If this is done properly, Jane will always be able to keep one hand on the spot and prevent Jack from slipping his hand in.

Contraction and Expansion

Contraction and expansion refers to the defender folding and opening, respectively, the arms across the body while executing each hand strike and then retracting the hand from the target area of the assailant's body. These movements facilitate the ability to execute subsequent strikes (due to the body coiling and releasing tension) that the defender anticipates using against the assailant. During the expansion phase, while one strike is making contact, the arm of the retracting hand is coiled, preparing to strike.

HAND COMBINATION 1: RAPID FRONT PUNCH

As the attacker gets closer and moves into critical distance, step forward and low with the left foot into a left front stance and execute a right punch to the attacker's groin. This defensive punch needs to occur prior to the aggressor being able to fully develop and deliver their offensive punch. Just after the right hand makes contact with the groin, replace the right hand punch with a left punch to the attacker's groin. Complete this punch combination by immediately using the right hand to strike the aggressor in the solar plexus with a hard punch, causing the aggressor to be propelled backward.

HAND COMBINATION 2: STOPPING THE CHARGE

As the assailant steps forward in preparation to throw a right-hand power punch, step forward with the left foot into a left front stance and execute a right palm heel strike to the chin of the aggressor. Follow this strike by punching the aggressor with a left punch to the rib cage immediately followed by a right elbow strike to the aggressor's head.

HAND COMBINATION 3: APPLAUSE PLEASE

Both hands simultaneously clap the assailant's ears. The left hand moves from the right side of the assailant's head to the center of the defender's chest, then strikes the assailant's face with an open left palm strike. The right hand strikes the assailant in the solar plexus, causing the assailant's upper body to bend forward. Pivot to a right front stance (in a clockwise direction) while executing a left elbow strike to the assailant's head.

HAND COMBINATION 4: WHAT GOES UP MUST COME DOWN

Begin by facing the assailant squarely and execute a right open hand palm strike to the left side of the assailant's face (this motion is the same as a forehand motion in tennis). Retract the right hand to the chest area, and then execute a right reverse hammer fist strike to the assailant's groin area. Move the right elbow up to execute a right upward elbow strike to the chin. Punch the assailant hard into the solar plexus with the left hand, causing the assailant to propel backward.

5

DEFENDING AGAINST HAND STRIKES

The techniques I describe in this chapter are not listed in any order of importance or priority. View them as you would items on a restaurant menu. Once you have gained proficiency in the techniques, nearly any combination can be selected. As an example, you can select a block with a certain counterstrike combination as a defense against a punch or select a different block (as long as the block covers the same area) with a different combination of strikes. You'll probably want to select a technique based on the potential injury the assailant will sustain. One technique might disable the assailant, stopping his incoming strike and rendering his striking arm inoperable, while another technique might render the assailant unconscious. Another factor in choosing one technique over another depends on the level of force the assailant is initiating. If the assailant presents deadly force, you might choose a technique where an expected result is death. Once you are faced with a threat, it's up to you to choose which technique and how much force to exert on an assailant.

When employing a self-defense technique, it is important to know exactly what areas of the assailant's body to strike and the optimum amount of the counterstrikes. Some areas of the assailant's body are more vulnerable than others, and strikes to these areas will affect the assailant in a variety of degrees. The targets outlined for each technique were selected for optimum effectiveness. Factors that a defender may consider when choosing one particular technique over another include personal taste in how the technique is constructed; the agility, strength, and flexibility the technique requires; how the defender's body structure fits with a particular technique; and the overall effect of the move itself. A defender who practices and gains proficiency in all of these techniques may find that movements from one technique may or may not be substituted into another. I have constructed the techniques listed in this text so that the defender's counterstrikes are optimized to inflict the greatest degree of pain within a given situation. Don't substitute movements from one technique to another, as changing any movement within any technique may substantially alter the outcome.

TIMING

Timing is critical when employing a self-defense technique. The following punch-timing drill can illustrate proper timing and assist the speed in the defender's technique. Assume a horse stance (pg. 43), with the left hand directly in front of the body to execute a front punch. Next, execute four rapid punches in succession, alternating hands with each punch. The time it takes to execute those four rapid punches should be the same time it takes to execute one block and three counterstrikes to the assailant. It should take only one breath to complete the defensive technique. The entire technique against one opponent should take from one to three seconds to complete.

DOMINANT HAND

Note which hand appears to be the aggressor's dominant side, as the attack is more likely to come from that side. About 90 percent of the population is naturally right-handed. When observing people, notice that they tend to manipulate tools, drinks, and writing instruments with their dominant hand. They also tend to wear wristwatches on their nondominant wrist.

For ease of explanation, the descriptions of the techniques depict the assailant striking with the right hand. To gain the most from these techniques, first practice them with the side of the body indicated in the descriptions. After gaining proficiency on that side, reverse each technique so that it counters an assailant striking with the left hand. This involves simply substituting left for right and vice versa.

STEPPING AND ANGLES OF ATTACK

An assailant has only two choices when stepping forward to initiate a hand strike: leading with either the dominant foot or the nondominant foot. For each of these options, the assailant can choose several directions in which to deliver a hand strike.

The assailant may step forward with the nondominant foot and execute a straight-line punch with the dominant hand. This movement offers the greatest amount of power to the assailant's punch because the hips undergo maximum rotation and the punch is delivered in a straight line. We'll call this type of punch a *straight punch*.

The strike may also come as the aggressor steps forward with the nondominant foot and executes a circular punch with the dominant hand. This position also offers a great amount of punching power because of the hip rotation. If this circular punch is delivered to the defender's head and maintains a consistent horizontal height, it is commonly referred to as a *roundhouse* or *haymaker* punch. If the circular punch is delivered downward to the defender's head, it is known as an *overhand* punch.

The assailant may also step forward with the dominant foot and strike with the dominant hand. The delivery can be either a straight punch, a roundhouse punch, or an overhand punch. This movement is commonly referred to as a *lunge* punch and does not have the power of the strikes described previously.

The last punching position is when the assailant steps with either foot and delivers the strike in a backhand motion. For example, the assailant places the right hand to his or her left shoulder, then moves that right hand in a backhand motion toward the defender's head, striking it with the back of the hand. This punching position is most commonly referred to as a *backhand strike*.

Although most of the defense techniques in this chapter will work effectively against the majority of hand strikes, some techniques will work better than others against certain types of hand strikes. The description of each technique indicates the single method of attack the assailant is initiating (straight punch, haymaker, backhand, etc.).

Also, for each technique a series of photographs illustrates the most critical portion of each technique. Not shown are the positions of the assailant and defender before the attack. In all cases, assume that the assailant was poised just outside critical distance and the defender was standing in a street-ready stance.

SELF-DEFENSE TIP

An assailant in the process of striking with the hand will first have to step out of the safety zone and inside critical distance. The assailant will plant his foot just seconds before executing the strike. The defender has two opportunities to launch a counterattack: the first is just as the assailant steps into critical distance but before the strike is fully deployed; and the second is after the assailant has deployed the strike, in which case the defender has to block the incoming strike and launch counterstrikes to stop any further acts of aggression.

DEFENDING AGAINST A STRAIGHT PUNCH

The following techniques work best when an assailant is stepping with the nondominant foot and initiating a straight punch with the dominant hand. For ease of explanation, the assailant's dominant side is designated as the right side.

REVERSE MOTIONS

As the assailant throws a right punch at the defender's head, the defender uses a rising block with the left hand while striking the assailant in the solar plexus with a right-hand punch. The defender then strikes the assailant with the left hand into the rib cage, immediately followed by a reverse hammer fist strike to the face.

BLOCK AND DOUBLE BACK

As the assailant executes a right punch to the head, use a right forearm block against the assailant's punch. Follow immediately with a right hammer fist to strike the assailant along the right side of the face. With the left hand, strike the assailant in the rib cage, followed by a right reverse knife hand strike to the right side of the assailant's neck. Step forward with the right foot into a right front stance while punching the assailant in the groin with the left hand.

PALM STRIKE TO FACE WITH TAKEDOWN

As the assailant strikes to the head, execute a left outer forearm block and a right palm heel strike to the assailant's chin. With the right leg, execute a right-leg takedown. This takedown is accomplished in the following manner: Place the calf of your right leg on the back of the assailant's right knee. As the palm heel strike moves the assailant's head backward, your right leg will move in the opposite direction the palm heel strike is moving the assailant. These movements done at the same time cause the assailant to fall onto his back. Immediately follow the takedown with a right stomp kick.

BLOCK WITH REVERSE KNIFE HAND TO GROIN

As the assailant throws a right punch at the defender's head, the defender uses a left outer forearm block and then steps forward with the left foot into a left front stance while deploying a right reverse knife hand strike to the right side of the assailant's neck. With the left hand, punch the assailant in the right side of the rib cage, followed by a right palm heel strike to the face. Execute a pivot to the right (into a right front stance) and strike the assailant with a left reverse knife hand strike to the groin. Last, use a left side kick to the assailant's torso.

MOVING OFF THE LINE

As the assailant begins to strike with a right-hand punch, block the incoming strike with a left forearm block and step forward with the left foot into a left front stance. Execute a right punch to the rib cage, followed by a right roundhouse kick (see chapter 6) to the groin. To control the assailant's punching arm, pull the arm downward as the right foot steps down. Transition to a right front stance and execute a left downward elbow strike to the assailant's upper spine area.

ELBOW DOWN, KNEE UP

As the assailant strikes with his or her right hand to the face, perform a left rising block and a right palm heel strike to the assailant's face. Complete a left punch to the ribs and a right reverse knife hand strike to the right side of the assailant's neck. Grab the assailant's neck with the right hand, pull it down (bending the assailant forward), and execute a left downward elbow strike to the top of the spine, followed by a left knee to the face and a left side kick to the knee of the forward leg.

BEATING THE PUNCH WITH
A QUADRUPLE KICK

As the assailant begins to strike to the face with his or her right hand, deploy a right side kick to the assailant's solar plexus, followed by a right roundhouse kick to the groin and a right roundhouse kick to the face. Step down with the right foot and execute a left front thrust kick (see chapter 6) to the groin with enough power to cause the assailant to be propelled backward.

KICK FIRST, THEN BLOCK

As the assailant moves into the defender's kicking range while attempting to carry out the attack, strike the assailant with a left front kick to the groin and block the incoming right hand strike with a left rising block. Immediately execute a left roundhouse kick to the inside of the left knee (the assailant's left knee should be forward). Step with the left foot so you are in the fighting guard stance directly in front of the assailant. Execute a snap punch with the right hand to the solar plexus, immediately followed by a right elbow strike to the assailant's head.

X BLOCK, RIB STRIKE, TAKEDOWN

Block the assailant's right punch with an X block, then execute a left reverse knife hand strike to the ribs and a right palm heel strike to the side of the face. As the assailant's body moves to an erect position, perform a right-leg takedown followed by a right kick to the assailant's rib cage.

BLOCK AND SIMULTANEOUS PECTORAL STRIKE

As the assailant strikes toward the defender's face with the right hand, use a right palm block and strike into the right side of the assailant's pectoral area with a left punch. With the right hand, complete a reverse knife hand strike to the ribs, and then deploy a left elbow strike to the face.

DEFENDING AGAINST A HAYMAKER PUNCH

Use the following four techniques to defend against a haymaker punch. This strike will probably be a power punch. Unlike a straight power punch, the delivery of the haymaker punch is circular in motion, much like the hook punch used in boxing. The assailant can step toward the defender with either foot.

KICK, BLOCK, AND HAMMER FIST TO FACE

As the assailant moves into the defender's kicking range while attempting to carry out the attack, strike the assailant with a right roundhouse kick to the solar plexus and block the incoming right-hand strike with a right forearm block. Execute a right reverse hammer fist strike to the assailant's face while stepping down with the right foot into a horse stance. Immediately strike the assailant's solar plexus with a left punch, then pivot and deploy a left front kick to the groin.

DOUBLE TAP TO THE EARS

Block the assailant's incoming right-hand strike with a left outer forearm block as the right hand strikes the assailant with a reverse knife hand strike to the ribs. Perform a right palm heel strike to the face followed by a right palm heel strike to the left ear followed by a left palm heel strike to the right ear. Execute a snap punch to the solar plexus, immediately followed by a left reverse knife hand strike to the throat. (These last two moves are a prime illustration of the contraction and expansion discussed in chapter 4.)

BLOCK AND DISABLE THE PUNCHING ARM

As the incoming strike approaches, perform a left outer forearm block and a right hammer fist strike to the biceps of the striking (right) arm while stepping with the right foot into a horse stance directly in front of the assailant. Execute a right elbow strike to the assailant's solar plexus in a reverse motion. With the left hand, hold onto the assailant's right wrist area. With the right hand, reach underneath the assailant's outstretched right arm and grab onto the right shoulder of the assailant. Execute a right-leg takedown, causing the assailant to land on his backside. The takedown position is accomplished in the following manner. Move the right foot to the outside of the assailant's right foot so that it faces the same direction of the assailant's right foot. Move the left foot to the outside of the assailant's left foot so that it too faces the same direction of the assailant's left foot. Once both feet are in position on the outsides of the assailant's feet, shift the hips and legs to that of a left front stance. (This position will have the left knee bent and the right knee straight.)

Now that the position is complete, the takedown is done by bending forward at the waist and touching the right elbow to the defender's left knee.

The assailant will be forced to fall over the top of your outstretched right leg. Although it appears there are a lot of movements required to gain this takedown position, with practice the movements from the elbow strike to the takedown position can be done in less than one second.

OUTER FOREARM BLOCK WITH
ELBOW STRIKE TO HEAD

While standing in the ready position, block the incoming strike with a left outer forearm block and immediately strike the assailant with a right palm heel strike to the face. Step forward with the right foot into a right front stance and execute a left punch to the solar plexus. Pivot to a left front stance and deploy a right elbow strike to the head.

DEFENDING AGAINST OVERHAND STRIKES

Use the following techniques to defend against a strike the assailant executes with his or her dominant hand at an almost downward angle. This strike (commonly called an overhand strike) literally moves downward toward the top of the defender's head.

X BLOCK, ELBOW BREAK WITH THROAT STRIKE

As the assailant begins to throw a punch, deploy a right front kick to the groin and then catch the incoming strike with an X block. Using the right hand, grab the assailant's right wrist and place the outer edge of your left arm against the outside of the assailant's right elbow area. Keeping equal pressure on the assailant's right elbow and wrist, force the arm to your

right side at approximately waist level, ensuring that the assailant's right arm stays horizontal. This is called the *arm bar* position, with the assailant bending forward at the waist. Quickly snap the arm by moving the wrist upward and elbow downward with your left arm, breaking the assail-ant's right elbow. Immediately deploy a right inverted knife hand strike to the assail-ant's throat.

BLOCK WITH ARMPIT STRIKE AND UPWARD CHIN TAP

Block the incoming strike with a left outer forearm block and strike with the right hand using a reverse knife hand strike to the right armpit. Step with the left foot into a left front stance. Pivot to the right into a right front stance and, using the left hand, punch into the solar plexus. Using the left hand again, perform a left upward palm strike to the chin (moving the assailant's face and head to an erect position). Pivot to a left front stance and execute a right punch to the assailant's groin.

STOPPING ATTACKS FROM ASSAILANT'S HAND AND FOOT

Use the following techniques against an assailant who is stepping with the dominant foot and striking with the dominant hand. These two techniques work best when the assailant steps forward with the right foot and executes a straight punch with the right hand.

BEATING THE PUNCH WITH A TRIPLE-KICK COMBINATION

As the assailant moves into the defender's kicking range while attempting to carry out the attack, strike the assailant with a right side kick to the solar plexus, followed by a right side kick to the assailant's right knee. Step down with the right foot turning to the left (counterclockwise) and execute a left back kick to the assailant's face.

ELBOW BREAK ACROSS WITH FOOT SWEEP

As the assailant strikes with the right hand to the head, use the left hand to execute a left forearm block and the right hand to execute a right forearm strike to the assailant's groin. The time between the block and strike will only be a fraction of a second. With the right hand, grab the assailant's right wrist and strike the assailant across the face with the left forearm. Simultaneously press the assailant's right elbow across your chest. By expanding your chest forward onto the assailant's elbow while at the same time pulling back on the assailant's right wrist and pressing your left forearm into the assailant's face, this will cause the assailant's right elbow to break.

The assailant will have their right foot between both of your feet with their weight shifting from their right foot toward their left foot. This weight shift occurs because of the preceding strikes causing injury and the aggressor will attempt to move away from the pain. While still

holding onto the assailant's right arm and with your left forearm across their face, the sweep is accomplished in the following manner. Move your left forearm into the face, forcing the aggressor's head to move backward and down. With your left foot, sweep the assailant's right foot. Visualize a sweep by using your left foot to pull the assailant's right foot along the ground. Once the assailant's upper body is forced backward at the same time their leg is pulled from underneath them, the result is for the assailant to fall backward.

OUTER FOREARM BLOCK WITH
ELBOW BREAK ACROSS

Block the assailant's incoming right-hand strike with a right outer forearm block. With the right hand, grab the assailant's right wrist, and place the outer edge of the left forearm against the assailant's right elbow. Keeping equal pressure on the assailant's right elbow and wrist, force the arm to your right side at approximately chst level, being sure to keep the right arm in that position both horizontally and vertically. Do not allow the assailant to bend over at the waist; keep his or her upper body erect. Quickly snapping the arm by moving the wrist and elbow toward each other, break the assailant's right elbow, and follow immediately with a right palm heel strike to the face. Take the assailant down with the right foot so that he or she falls onto the back. Refer to the takedown used in the Palm Strike to Face With Takedown (page 67 illustrates the take down). Follow with a right kick to the assailant's rib cage or head.

REVERSE WRISTLOCK TAKEDOWN

Block the incoming strike with a left forearm block and grab the assailant's right wrist with your right hand in a reverse wrist lock position. (To achieve a reverse wrist lock, reach over the top of the assailant's punch with your right hand and place your right thumb on the back of his hand while placing the fingers of the right hand on the fleshy portion of his right hand. Strike the assailant with an elbow strike to the rib cage in a reverse motion. Step under the assailant's outstretched arm with the left foot and execute a reverse wrist lock takedown using both hands. The takedown is performed by rotating your hands in a counterclockwise direction, forcing the assailant to land on his back on the ground. Finish with a left stomp kick to the head.

Lateral Movement Techniques

Lateral movement involves simply blocking an assailant's strike and almost simultaneously moving to the side or rear of the assailant. This type of movement can be of great benefit in that it places the defender in a position to maximize striking ability while at the same time minimizing the assailant's ability to strike. To begin, the defender must first block the incoming strike. The defender may then move to a position of advantage and return counterstrikes to the assailant.

In some of the techniques in this book, the defender blocks the incoming strike and returns counterstrikes to the anterior, or front, of the assailant. Although these types of defensive techniques can be very successful, the techniques that provide the greatest opportunity for the defender's safety are those that move the assailant to a position of disadvantage and the defender to a position of advantage.

Defensive lateral moves mandate that the defender employ a block that closes up the assailant. After employing the block, the defender moves to the position of advantage. The footwork the defender uses depends on the relative position of the feet at the beginning of the technique.

If you're standing in a street-ready position, the footwork for the lateral movement involves either stepping with one foot and the body to 90 or 45 degrees in one direction. If the assailant uses the right hand to strike at your head while stepping with the left leg, you can block the aggressor's punch with a right outer forearm block, thereby closing off the assailant from any immediate hand strikes. You will only need to step forward with the left foot at a 45-degree angle to gain access to the right lateral and posterior side of the aggressor. If the assailant uses the same right hand punch, however, choosing to step forward with the right leg, you'll need only to move sideways with your left foot at a 90-degree angle to gain access to the right lateral and posterior side of the aggressor.

The concept also applies if the defender and the assailant have both assumed a fighting stance. For example, if the defender has assumed a stance with the left foot forward and the assailant moves with his or her left foot forward, the defender will block with the left hand to close up the assailant. The defender moves the right foot forward by approximately 90 degrees and delivers counterstrikes to the left lateral side and left posterior of the assailant. The defender's right foot, which was to the rear and farther away from the assailant, is the foot that has to move farther in this lateral movement—about 30 inches or so.

To counter a left punch to the face, the defender blocks with the left outer forearm and executes a right punch to the assailant's left rib cage. The defender then moves the right foot forward by 45 degrees. As the right foot touches the ground, the defender strikes using the left hand in a reverse knife hand strike to the assailant's left kidney area. The defender

Lateral movement positions for blocking a left punch to the face.

uses the right hand to strike the assailant in the small of the back and then executes a right front kick to the assailant's groin from behind.

If your stance has the right foot forward and the assailant moves with his or her left foot forward, you'll block with the right hand to close up the assailant. The defender's footwork involves moving the right foot forward about 45 degrees and delivering counterstrikes to the left lateral side and left posterior of the assailant. The defender's right foot, which was the front foot before the attack, will move only a slight distance compared to the previous position.

The defender blocks a left punch to the face with the right palm and executes a left punch to the assailant's rib cage. The defender moves the right foot about 45 degrees to the right to step behind the assailant. As the right foot touches the ground, the defender strikes into the assailant's left kidney area with a right punch. The defender then deploys a right roundhouse kick into the back of the assailant's left knee (to facilitate bending the assailant's upper body backward), followed by a left elbow strike to the assailant's face.

6

KICKS

In self-defense, the ability to use the legs when applying kicks is just as vital as skill with the hands. Because of the extreme difficulty involved in controlling the large muscles of the leg, the defender must invest adequate time to learn, practice, and finally execute each kick correctly.

An effective combination of kicks or kicks combined with hand strikes can have a devastating effect on an assailant and can result in terminating the threat much sooner. As with using hand strikes to fend off an assailant, the defender must have a thorough understanding of the dynamics of kicking to be accurate and effective. Kicking also requires one unique prerequisite that punching does not: proper balance. A defender who neglects to maintain balance when applying any kick may wind up flat on the floor.

Balance while kicking consists of three essential elements: the supporting foot, the supporting knee, and the position of the body over the supporting leg during the kick. The supporting foot is the foot not involved in the kick, and it must be positioned flat on the ground.

Standing on any other portion of the foot (such as the ball, the heel, or the outside edge) will not support balance. The supporting knee must be sufficiently bent to absorb any potential shock from the kick as well as to allow the body to flow smoothly through the kicking movement. The position of the body over the supporting leg during the kick varies from kick to kick. The front kick is the only kick in which the upper torso remains erect. With all the other kicks, the upper torso needs to move slightly away from the kick itself. In all kicks, the upper torso must anticipate the contact with the desired target and compensate for the incoming force.

This chapter presents four basic kicks, each designed to deliver force quickly to a vulnerable target area. Each kick requires correct components such as form, foot position, focus (or accuracy), balance, and eye-foot coordination, all of which are essential to successfully executing a kick to a desired target. There are four steps to each kick. The kick will lift from the floor with the kicking ankle next to the supporting knee, extend, retract, and return to the floor.

Never allow the knee of the kicking leg to straighten out while kicking. The kicking knee should always have a small amount of bend in the knee to absorb any potential shock from impact and to prevent hyper-extension of the kicking knee joint. Kicking with any degree of speed combined with totally straightening the knee allows the knee to hyper-extend, which will cause substantial damage to the knee after repeated kicks.

Practice each kick slowly at first to learn the proper form. Add other components such as speed and power only after achieving proficiency over each kick. One of the last components to add to the practice routine is a target. Before actually striking a target, make sure the kick is correct in focus (the ability to place the kick exactly on the spot the strike is intended to make contact) and in control (the degree to which contact is made with the target). These other components are essential; otherwise the risk of injury is very high.

Targets that are ideal to use when practicing kicks are as follows. First, perform kicks in the air without a tangible target to ensure the kick will have the proper form and focus. Second, using kite string suspend a foam ball to a comfortable height (about waist level). Using the foam ball, slowly execute each kick only to stop about one inch short of hitting the ball. The knee of the kicking foot should still be slightly bent. The kick should be able to go directly to the same spot each time it is executed. Gradually add speed to the kick until you can execute it at full speed.

Other practice targets include a practice partner. The kicks would be delivered to the intended targets and should stop approximately one inch shy of actually striking the target. Again, keep the kicking knee slightly bent to absorb any potential shock and to prevent hyper-extension of the knee joint.

Kicking also requires dexterity in both legs. The ability to be ambidextrous in kicking requires conscious practice, with significant repetitions of each kick with both legs.

A defender may deliver kicks to an aggressor in one of two angles: direct, which some refer to as linear, or indirect, also referred to as circular. The appropriate angle to use in a particular situation depends on the threat the aggressor is presenting and the effect the defender wishes to achieve. If the aggressor is charging into the defender, the defender must use a direct-angle kick to stop the aggressor's forward momentum. The front kick, side kick, and back kicks are all direct-angle kicks. Once an aggressor's forward momentum has been suspended, an indirect kick may be used. The roundhouse kick is delivered in a circular motion and for that reason is classified as an indirect-angle kick.

Never depend on just one kick (or one hand strike) to completely stop an attack. A self-defense technique should always rely on a combination of movements to render an attacker incapable of further aggression. The degree of injury that kicks can inflict on an attacker can range from moderate discomfort to broken bones and even to death.

STRIKING AREAS OF THE FOOT

Four basic areas of the foot can make contact with the intended target area of the assailant's body during execution of a kick: the instep, the ball of the foot, the outside edge of the foot (referred to as knife edge), and the heel. Each kick is designed to use one of these areas. Using the wrong part of the foot can result in the defender breaking their own foot while delivering a kick.

The front kick uses only the instep and ball of the foot, depending on whether the kick will connect with soft tissue or a harder surface. As an example, when the front kick is delivered to the groin underneath the legs, the instep may be used. However, if the front kick will come into contact with the solar plexus, the ball of the foot must be the kicking contact surface. If the toes of the kicking foot make contact while kicking, the toes will break.

The roundhouse kick may employ the instep of the foot only when the kick is delivered to the torso. When the roundhouse kick is executed to the head, groin, or solar plexus, the ball of the foot must be used. Because the roundhouse kick is delivered to the groin while in front of the assailant, the instep cannot be used.

The side kick uses only the outside edge (knife edge) of the foot, and the back kick uses the heel.

When executing a kick, use only the specific striking areas of the foot designated for each kick. Practice kicking with the specific striking areas of the foot without wearing shoes. When shoes are added, note if the shoes are pliable enough when delivering a front kick. Most tennis shoes are pliable enough to expose the ball of the foot for front and roundhouse kicks. Many other street shoes may not have the same flexibility. If the shoes cannot bend enough to use the ball of the foot, consider using another kick rather than risk injury to the foot. For the side kick and back kick, all shoes should be capable of exposing this portion of the foot.

Kicking Directions

In self-defense, as in life in general, using the best tool at the appropriate time produces the best result. With kicks, consider the direction in which to deploy the kick to achieve the best results. Kicking in the wrong direction will not only drastically reduce the kick's effectiveness but may also cause injury to the kicker. When deployed with the right leg, the four kicks (front kick, roundhouse kick, side kick, and back kick), will cover 180 degrees on one side of the body. Moving clockwise to the left side of the body, the four kicks deployed by the left leg (back kick, side kick, roundhouse kick, and front kick) will cover the remaining 180 degrees. Use clock positions to determine appropriate kick direction.

- Starting with the right leg, the front kick covers from 12 o'clock to 1 o'clock, the roundhouse kick covers from 1 o'clock to 3 o'clock, the side kick covers from 3 o'clock to 5 o'clock, and the back kick covers from 5 o'clock to 6 o'clock.
- With the left leg, the back kick covers from 6 o'clock to 7 o'clock, the left side kick covers from 7 o'clock to 9 o'clock, the left roundhouse kick covers from 9 o'clock to 11 o'clock, and the left front kick covers from 11 o'clock to 12 o'clock.

Kicking Effects

The two types of kicking effects are snap kicks and thrust kicks. A snap kick is performed with a quicker move and will only press about two inches into the assailant's body. The result to the assailant from a snap kick is that only the immediate area where the kick makes contact moves. For example, when a snap kick is executed to an attacker's groin, the attacker's upper body bends slightly forward while the groin area moves slightly away from the direction of the kick.

The thrust kick is designed to move through the target. Not only does the immediate area where the kick makes contact move, but the assailant's entire body is forced backward. For example, when a thrust kick is executed to an attacker's groin, the attacker's upper body will bend forward at the waist and the attacker's entire body is propelled backward.

Another way of looking at the effect of a snap kick versus that of a thrust kick is that the snap kick will affect the assailant but will leave his or her body in position for the defender to deploy follow-up strikes. A thrust kick forces the assailant away, creating more distance and taking away the potential for immediate follow-up strikes.

FRONT KICK

A front kick is best suited for use against an aggressor positioned directly in front of the defender. The front kick should be limited to two surfaces on the defender's foot: the ball of the foot (used when kicking hard targets such as the torso) and the instep (used only when kicking the groin from underneath and between the legs of the assailant). Using any other part of the foot for this kick may seriously injure the defender.

Begin by standing with the feet approximately shoulder-width apart (step 1). Lift the kicking foot so the ankle is next to (but not touching) the supporting knee (step 2). Extend the kicking leg at the knee, moving the foot forward (step 3). Retract the foot and return the foot so the kicking ankle is adjacent to the supporting knee (step 2). Return the kicking foot to the floor so the feet are again approximately shoulder-width apart (step 1).

Steps 2 and 3 of the front kick.

ROUNDHOUSE KICK

The target direction of the roundhouse kick is either 90 degrees to the side or 45 degrees to the front. The kicking surface is the ball of the foot. Lift the kicking foot so that the ankle is next to the supporting knee. As the kicking leg extends toward the target, allow the supporting foot to rotate outward. Retract the kicking leg back into the coiled position. Return the kicking foot back to the ground. Ideal targets for this kick are the knee, groin, torso, and head.

SIDE KICK

Of all the basic kicks, the side kick is probably the most difficult kick to master. This kick can produce a significant amount of power. The target direction is 90 degrees to the side of the defender. The kicking surface is the knife edge portion of the foot. The knife edge can best be described while standing barefoot on a floor. Simply stated, the knife edge is the area on the outside edges of both feet between the heels and continues along the sides where the edge stops approximately two inches before reaching the little toes of each foot.

Begin by lifting the kicking leg with the knee pointed as directly as possible toward the intended target and the kicking foot adjacent to the supporting knee. The toes of the supporting foot align with and point in the same direction as the toes of the supporting foot to as great a degree as the kicker's flexibility allows. Extend the kick in the direction of the target. Prior to contact being made, ensure the kicking foot is in a knife edge position (refer to the earlier explanation of knife edge position). This position allows a greater degree of control over the kick so the defender may place it where it will cause the most damage to the aggressor. Using any other portion of the foot for this kick will alter its overall effectiveness, change the dynamic of the kick, needlessly injure the defender as the kick makes contact with the target, or any combination of these. Retract the kicking foot and then replace that foot on the floor. Ideal targets for a side kick are the knees, thighs, torso and head.

BACK KICK

The direction of this kick is 180 degrees directly behind the defender. The kicking surface is the heel. Begin by raising the kicking knee forward and placing the kicking ankle adjacent to the supporting knee in the same manner as for the front kick. Extend the kicking leg directly backward while looking back over the shoulder on that side toward the intended target (e.g., when kicking with the left leg, look back over the left shoulder). Retract the kicking leg back to the initial lift position (kicking ankle next to the supporting knee). Return the kicking foot to the ground.

During the kick, the defender's upper body moves in the opposite direction of the kick to compensate for the shift in balance (see photos). Return the upper body to an upright position while recoiling the foot from the target. Position the kicking foot so that the toes face outward at 45 degrees. Positioning the foot at this angle gives the kicker a greater degree of comfort and prevents injury to the muscles of the kicking leg. Ideal targets for this kick include the torso and in some cases (such as when a kicker has excellent eye-foot coordination) the head.

Developing Kicks

Because kicking involves so many muscles, be sure to complete proper warm-up and stretching techniques before attempting any kick. Practice kicks in front of a mirror to observe the form. Perform all kicks slowly to ensure form and balance before adding speed to any kick.

Eye-foot coordination is crucial to effective kicking. Most people are accustomed to using their hands to touch the things their eyes see and find it more difficult to train their feet to do the same thing. Effective kicking requires diligent practice kicking to a specific focal point that is not always static or stationary. Targets are sometimes mobile, and kicking a mobile target develops the eye-foot coordination that will be critical in real-life defense situations. One of the best training methods for developing this coordination is kicking a small foam ball (about the size of a softball). Because of its soft construction, the ball will not damage any surface it comes into contact with, such as glass, furniture, or other self-defense practitioners.

Start by suspending the foam ball by a string from the ceiling. Adjust it to various heights and execute a variety of kicks to it. Next, hold the ball and throw it into the air. As the ball falls, kick it using the basic kicks from this chapter. The kicker should be capable of kicking equally well with either leg, using all the kicks described in this chapter, and making solid contact with the ball on each kick.

Another alternative is to have another person launch the ball into the air. Again, use all the kicks to make solid contact with the ball, literally kicking it back to the person who threw it.

To develop speed for all kicks, start slow and gradually increase speed only after gaining proficiency in the proper mechanics and fundamentals, paying special attention to the exact foot position of each kick. Practicing kicks and hand strikes involves two distinct types of speed: mental speed and physical speed. Mental speed is the fastest speed that is humanly possible for a particular movement. This speed is often perceived as much faster than actual physical speed. Physical speed is the exact speed of the human body while it is actually performing a particular movement. The goal is to picture mental speed, then match actual physical speed to it. Performing this mental exercise will increase physical speed.

Power is a natural by-product of correct body mechanics and speed of movement. There is no need to kick trees or light poles to develop kicking power. Kicking inanimate targets will only produce negative results and create significant injuries to the body in later years. Never attempt to kick with too much power. Using power kicks at an inappropriate time telegraphs the kick.

KICKING ERRORS

The defender must guard against overextending the kick. If the kick is extended past the leg's natural range of motion, the defender will lose balance and wind up in a position that is disadvantageous for self-defense.

Beware of hyperextending the knee joint while kicking. This hyperextension occurs when the kicking knee and leg are locked straight. It is imperative for the defender to keep the knee of the kicking leg slightly bent to absorb the shock of the kick. Using the proper form for each specific kick can easily correct kicking errors. Pay strict attention to detail while practicing so that you develop the appropriate muscle memory for each kick.

Never let your leg linger after a kick. Leaving the leg extended allows the aggressor to grab hold of it, changing the overall effectiveness of the movement. Also realize that in certain situations it may not be practical to use kicks against an aggressor. If the defender is standing on an icy or extremely slippery surface, lifting the leg to kick may cause the defender to wind up flat on the ground. Also, using a kick to defend against an assailant in a close, confined space such as the inside of a bathroom stall or the interior of a car is not possible.

As with hand strikes, a defender needs to be a certain distance away from the assailant for a kick to achieve its maximum effect. This distance is the maximum allowed in which a defender may stand away from the aggressor and still be capable of delivering an effective kick—approximately six inches less than the defender's total leg reach. To measure this distance, if the defender extended the leg toward the aggressor, the aggressor would be standing just six inches inside of that full leg's reach. A kick executed when the aggressor is standing too close to the defender will be jammed and ineffective.

A kick executed when the aggressor is standing outside the maximum effective range will be overextended and thereby ineffective. When a kick is overextended, the kicker is in a very precarious position. Not only is the kick virtually ineffective, but the kicker is out of position and incapable of immediately following up with any other viable technique. For maximum effectiveness, the kick requires the full distance to develop.

The defender also must anticipate the movement of the aggressor in direct relation to the impact of the kick. When using a kick to defend against an aggressor who is charging forward, the defender must execute the kick while maintaining balance and compensating for the force of the charging aggressor.

Two methods are helpful in developing this ability: practicing kicks against a heavy bag, and practicing against an actual charging opponent in a controlled environment. Heavy bags are available in nearly every sporting goods store that sells boxing equipment. Hanging the heavy bag requires sufficient support to not only hold the weight of the bag, but also to compensate for the force of the swinging heavy bag.

Start by kicking the middle of the heavy bag when the bag is stationary. Assume a horse stance and fighting guard up with the left side facing the heavy bag. This initial position (the horse stance) will be about three feet from the chest to the heavy bag. Slide the right (rear) foot up to and alongside the left foot. Lift the left side kick and kick the middle of the bag. Perform the kick with the foot closest to the heavy bag. Adjust your distance so the kick can strike the bag while you're extending your kicking leg as far as you can. Ensure the kicking knee never fully straightens out or overextends. Practice the kick with both the left and right leg.

Next, give the heavy bag a slight push away from the direction of the kicker. Wait for the bag to begin moving toward you before you step up with the supporting foot to execute the kick with the leg closest to the heavy bag. Gradually increase the swing of the heavy bag from a slight push to that of a full push, with the bag moving to almost a horizontal position as it swings away. When the bag begins to move toward you, wait until the last possible moment and then step up with the supporting foot to execute a more powerful side kick with the leg closest to the heavy bag. The goal here is to stop the momentum of the heavy bag by kicking it at a full speed and full range of motion without the bag's force knocking you off balance.

The second practice method involves kicking an actual opponent who is practicing techniques with you. It's important to control the amount of power delivered in each kick so as not to injure the opponent. As you stand in a street-ready position, your opponent moves from a safety zone into the critical distance zone to strike you. You execute the side kick to the torso area of your opponent, taking great care not to injure him or her. The kick should be delivered at full speed and should stop just a fraction of an inch shy of striking the opponent.

OTHER KICKS

A variety of other kicks exist. They are, however, merely derivatives of the four basic kicks (front, roundhouse, side, and back) and employ slightly different motions during delivery.

Aerial kicks require the defender to leave the ground and execute a kick while both feet are in the air. Keep in mind that this factor adds extreme vulnerability. If the aerial kicker's balance is upset during the application of the kick, the assailant can take the kicker violently to the ground simply by pushing the defender while airborne. Leaping into the air to execute a kick may provide the advantage of surprise, but the disadvantages far outweigh the advantages.

In spinning kicks, the kicker momentarily turns 180 degrees while delivering the kick. This movement also requires the defender to momentarily turn his or her back to the aggressor while executing the kick. If the aggressor is able to exploit this moment of vulnerability and strike the defender to his or her back, backside, or back of the head, the results could be devastating to the defender.

These exotic kicks can be flashy, but they require advanced skills and years of practice to master. It can be dangerous to use these types of kicks without first developing the requisite ability, knowledge of when to use them, and skill to pull them off successfully. Using any exotic kick in actual combat without first obtaining the proficiency necessary to perform it can have disastrous results.

Double or triple kicks are multiple kicks executed with the same leg before it returns to the floor. In some systems, the first kick of a double-kick combination is used to fake out the aggressor so that the second kick is more effective. I believe, however, that with double or triple kicks, the first kick should not be a fake; all kicks should make contact with their intended target. If a person is going to go through the effort of moving, don't waste a move; strike the aggressor with each possible move. There is also a possibility that when a movement is done, if the assailant is not effected by the strike, he may be able capitalize on the fact that a movement by the defender did not strike nor cause injury to them and that may provide them the chance to strike and cause injury.

When given the opportunity to strike an assailant with multiple kicks, use each kick wisely, making contact with each kick. To minimize the time between kicks, do not fully retract the kicking leg after executing the first kick. Instead, retract the kicking leg only far enough from the aggressor's body to execute the subsequent kicks.

KICKING COMBINATIONS

As with hand strikes, kicks should be used in combinations designed to incapacitate the aggressor. These combinations can consist of kicks with the same leg, kicks with alternating legs, or a combination of the two. In order to perform multiple kicks with the same leg, perform a right roundhouse kick to the groin followed by a right roundhouse kick to the solar plexus. An example of kicking with alternating legs would consist of a left side kick to the assailant's knee, right front kick to the chest followed by a left side kick to the assailant's solar plexus. Kicking with a combination of the two would have the defender using a right roundhouse kick to the groin and a right roundhouse kick to the solar plexus followed by a left side kick to the knee, right front kick to the chest, followed by a left side kick to the solar plexus.

Keep in mind that even though the technique makes use of multiple kicks, hand techniques incorporated into the technique provide an even greater opportunity to incapacitate the aggressor.

KICK COMBINATION 1: WALK ON BY

This combination requires the kicker to alternate legs with each kick, as in walking forward. Execute a right front snap kick to the aggressor's solar plexus and a left front snap kick to the groin. Then execute a right side snap kick to the aggressor's chest followed by a left side thrust kick to the knee of the forward leg.

KICK COMBINATION 2: ALL FROM ONE

All of these kicks are done with the same leg. Execute a right front snap kick to the groin and a right roundhouse kick to the aggressor's solar plexus, followed by a right side kick to the knee of the aggressor's forward leg. When executing multiple kicks with the same leg, recoil the kicking leg from the target only as far back as the knee before executing the next kick. The kicking foot returns to the ground only upon completion of the third kick.

KICK COMBINATION 3: INSIDE OUT

The kicks in this technique alternate from left foot to right foot, and then again to the left foot. As the assailant rushes in and begins to strike with a right hand punch to the face, use a left side kick to the abdomen, hard enough to stop their forward momentum. (The immediate reaction of the assailant is that he will be stopped in his tracks and his body is slightly bending forward at the waist) Step down with the left foot and turn one quarter turn to the right. Look over the right shoulder and execute a right back kick to the assailant's face. Step down with the right foot and toward the assailant, continuing to turn to the right. As the assailant begins to fall backward, execute a left front kick to the groin.

KICK COMBINATION 4:
THREE STRIKES, YOU'RE OUT

This combination requires the kicker to alternate legs with each kick. Just as the assailant steps into range to deliver a right hand punch and before the punch is halfway to its intended target, execute a right side kick to the left knee, causing the assailant to bend forward at the waist. Step down with the right foot and deliver a left front kick to the solar plexus. Immediately use a right front kick to the aggressor's groin.

7

DEFENDING
AGAINST KICKS

The actual skill level of aggressors who attempt to kick is usually very low. These aggressors may have participated in one or two martial arts classes, or perhaps they have watched a number of martial arts movies and try to imitate those moves. Their kicks are usually done to gross imperfection, and a defender can easily observe, block, and effectively counter them. As with any defensive technique, the first task is to block the aggressive movement, and the second is to counter the strike by delivering immediate and intense pain to the aggressor, rendering him or her incapable of any subsequent attack.

The techniques outlined in this chapter are designed for use against an aggressor who is attempting to kick. Just as in defending against hand strikes, the defender stands in a street-ready stance and transitions through the various defensive positions and stances that will facilitate the delivery of effective counterstrikes to the aggressor.

The techniques I describe in this chapter are not listed in any order of importance or priority. As in chapter 5, these self-defense techniques can be chosen as you would select items from a restaurant menu. Once you're proficient in the techniques, nearly any combination can be selected. As an example, you can use a block with a certain counterstrike combination as a defense against a kick or perform a different block (as long as the block covers the same area) with a different combination of strikes. In many cases, you'll select your technique based on the degree of potential injury the assailant will sustain. One self-defense technique might disable the assailant, stopping his incoming strike and rendering his striking leg inoperable, while another technique might render the assailant unconscious. Another factor to consider when choosing one technique over another is the level of force the assailant is initiating. If the assailant presents a risk of deadly force, you might choose a technique where the expected result is death. Once faced with a threat, it's up to you to choose which technique to employ and how much force to exert on your assailant.

For ease of explanation, unless otherwise noted, the descriptions of the techniques are for defending against an aggressor kicking with the right leg. To gain the most from these techniques, first practice them with the side of the body indicated in the descriptions. After gaining proficiency on that side, reverse each technique so that it counters an assailant kicking with the left leg. This involves simply substituting left for right and vice versa.

As mentioned in chapter 5, the factors that a defender may consider when choosing one technique over another include personal taste in technique construction; the agility, strength, and flexibility the technique requires; how the defender's body structure fits with a particular technique; and the overall effect of the move itself on the assailant. Just as with defending against hand strikes, a defender who practices and gains proficiency in all of these techniques may find that movements from one technique may or may not be substituted into another. I have constructed the techniques listed in this text so that the defender's counterstrikes are optimized to inflict the greatest degree of pain within a given situation. You can substitute movements from one technique to another, but be aware that changing any movement within any technique may substantially alter the outcome.

SELF-DEFENSE TIP

An aggressor attempting to kick a defender will move from the safety zone and into critical distance for kicking, which is slightly farther away from the defender than critical distance for punching. An assailant planning to kick will plant the foot of the support (nonkicking) leg in a position that is farther away from the defender than the lead foot would be planted if the assailant were planning a hand strike. This is because a strike with the leg must travel a greater distance to its target than a strike with the arm. After planting the support foot, the assailant will then lift the kicking leg and begin to deliver the kick.

Just as in chapter 5, a series of photographs illustrate the most critical portion of each technique. Not shown are the positions of the aggressor and the defender before the attack. In all cases, assume that the aggressor was poised just outside critical distance and the defender was standing in a street-ready stance.

DEFENDING AGAINST A FRONT KICK

A front kick is usually thrown at the lower part of the body. Although it can be directed at any target, most aggressors choose the knees, groin, or torso.

ACHILLES STOMP

As the assailant throws a right front kick at the groin, block the kick with a right downward block turning the assailant. (Whenever a hard forceful kick is thrown and is deflected, the block will in effect turn the assailant, in this case exposing the back of the aggressor). With the right foot, triple kick the assailant by placing a right front kick to the groin delivered from behind the assailant and underneath his or her kicking leg. When the assailant's kicking leg touches the ground, place a side kick into the outside of their right knee, followed by a right front stomp on the assailant's right Achilles tendon.

INNER KNEE BREAKDOWN WITH
BACK KICK TO FACE

As the assailant deploys a right front kick, execute a left downward block. The assailant's kicking foot should land approximately two feet away from the defender's left foot at about a 45-degree angle to the front and left. Kick the assailant in the groin with a left front kick, followed by a left side snap kick to the inside of the assailant's right knee. Step down with the left foot and execute a back thrust kick with the right foot to the assailant's face.

KNEE BREAK AND KICK INTO GROIN

As the assailant deploys a right front kick, use a right wrist block to block the incoming kick. After the block makes contact, grab the assailant's right (kicking) foot and hold onto it with both hands. Execute a right front kick to the assailant's groin and a right side kick to the knee of the assailant's left (supporting) leg. With the right foot, assist in the takedown by using a roundhouse kick to the assailant's torso. With the right leg, step over the assailant's right leg and step down. At this point, the assailant should be on his or her backside. Sit down over the right knee to break it, then stand up with your back to the assailant and follow with a left back kick to the assailant's groin.

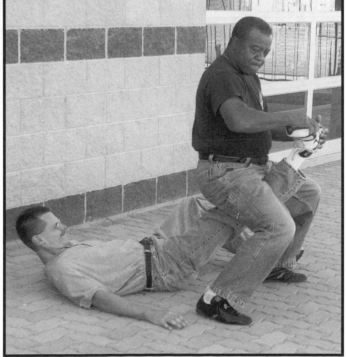

BLOCK AND TRIPLE KICK COMBINATION

Block the incoming right front kick with a right wrist block and kick the assailant in the groin with the right foot. As the assailant's right foot touches the ground, execute a right roundhouse kick to the inside of the assailant's right knee. Deploy a right side thrust kick to the torso.

LEG SCOOP, SWEEP, AND STOMP KICK

As the assailant kicks with the right front kick, execute a right downward block. With the right hand, scoop the assailant's right leg, cupping the leg at the knee into your arm. With your left foot, sweep the assailant's left foot. (This is easily done because the assailant is standing on one foot and you will have altered his balance once his right leg is captured.) The left foot sweep is accomplished by moving his foot along the ground with your left foot by about 12 inches. Follow with a left stomp kick to the assailant's head.

Defending Against a Side Kick

Targets for side kicks usually range from the knee to the torso. A skillful kicker, however, can place this kick at head level.

WRIST BLOCK, FOOT SWEEP, AND STOMP KICK TO BACK OF HEAD

As the assailant throws a right side kick at the torso, use a right wrist block with the left arm to assist in trapping the assailant's right leg. While still holding onto the assailant's leg, execute a right side kick to the groin. Position the assailant's foot directly in front of the body while simultaneously checking their right arm from movement and executing a left punch to the torso. With the right foot, sweep the assailant's right foot so the assailant falls face forward, then execute a right stomp kick to the back of the assailant's head.

WRIST BLOCK, FOOT SWEEP, AND STOMP KICK TO FACE

As the assailant throws a left side kick at the torso, use a right wrist block to block the kick. Immediately place the left hand on top of the blocked kick to capture the assailant's left foot, followed by a right front kick to the groin Step towards the assailant with the right foot and assume a horse stance. Place your right hand over the left arm of the assailant to negate any potential strike with their left hand and execute a left punch to their kidney. The right foot will sweep the assailant's left leg, causing the assailant to fall backward. Execute a left stomp to the assailant's head.

WRIST BLOCK, STRIKE TO GROIN, AND ELBOW STRIKE

Block the assailant's left side kick with a left wrist block, followed by a left front kick to the groin. Place your left hand over the left arm of the assailant to negate any potential strike with his left hand and execute a right punch to his kidney, followed by a right elbow strike to his head.

KNEE BREAKDOWN,
ROUNDHOUSE KICK TO FACE

When the assailant throws a right side kick toward the torso, block the kick with a right downward block and execute a right front kick to the groin. As the assailant's right foot touches the ground, execute a right side kick to the back of the right knee, followed immediately by a right roundhouse kick to the face.

DEFENDING AGAINST A ROUNDHOUSE KICK

The target area of a roundhouse kick usually ranges from the groin to the head. In most instances, inexperienced kickers throw these kicks into the torso area.

CROSS-BODY BLOCK, TAKEDOWN, AND GROIN STOMP

As the assailant throws a right roundhouse kick into the body, block it with both a left downward block and a right forearm block. Once contact is made, move the left arm (which is in the lower position of the block) upward to trap the assailant's right leg. With the right foot, execute a takedown by sweeping the assailant's left supporting leg. With the right foot, stomp kick into the fallen assailant's groin.

KNEE ROLLOVER TAKEDOWN

When the assailant throws a right roundhouse kick, use a right forearm block and with the left hand, grab the assailant's right leg at the calf. Deploy a right side kick to the groin, then a right side kick to the supporting knee. Execute the takedown by rotating and pressing the assailant's right knee toward the ground so the assailant falls facedown. While the assailant's hands are occupied in reaching for the ground, execute a left front kick to the body and a right front kick to the face.

KNEE WRENCH TAKEDOWN

Block the incoming kick with a left outer forearm block and catch the kicking foot with the right hand. Follow immediately with a right side kick to the groin. Wrench the assailant's ankle by twisting it counter-clockwise and up. As the assailant falls onto his or her backside, execute a left stomp kick to the head.

8

BREAKING
HOLDS AND
DEFENDING
AGAINST
WEAPONS

Effective self-defense requires that the defender know not only how to defend against hand strikes and kicks, but also how to break free when an aggressor is grabbing and holding onto the body. The situations presented here depict some of the common ways an aggressor holds onto a defender and describe techniques to break these holds. With each of these techniques, the defender breaks free and employs countermeasures to ensure that the aggressor does not continue further acts of aggression.

BEAR HUG FROM REAR WITH ARMS FREE

Make a fist with the right hand, but slightly release the middle finger of that hand so the knuckle protrudes. Since the defender's arms are not restricted, use the right hand to strike the back of the assailant's hand with the protruded knuckle. (The hand that will be struck is whichever hand of the assailant's is on top) Pry the top hand away and execute a reverse wrist lock takedown. The takedown action if done in a quick snapping motion will break the assailant's wrist. After the assailant has fallen, use a front kick to the face.

BEAR HUG FROM REAR WITH ARMS PINNED

Pry the assailant's extended hand from its grip. Step into a horse stance (pg. 43) on the side of the pried hand, apply a reverse vertical wristlock and secure the elbow, then deploy a side kick to the knee.

BEAR HUG FROM FRONT WITH ARMS FREE

Using the palms of both hands, strike both the assailant's ears in a clapping motion. Strike the assailant along both sides of his neck with both hands in knife hand strikes immediately followed with a knee strike to the groin. Place the right hand at the back of the assailant's head (at the crown of his head) and the left palm on his chin. Take the assailant down by quickly twisting his head in a clockwise direction and down to the right. After the assailant has landed, execute a left front kick to the face.

BEAR HUG FROM FRONT WITH ARMS PINNED

Use both hands to form a knife-hand position and strike the rib cage of the assailant. Pry the assailant's arms free. This is done by rotating both elbows upward and outward. Execute a hip throw. A hip throw is performed by putting the right hand and arm around the waist area of the assailant, as in hugging. Allow the left hand to grab the assailant's right arm. Move both feet 180 degrees to face the same direction as the assailant's feet. Bend the knees to lower the hips about 12 to 16 inches. Simultaneously move the hips 10 inches to the right. (With practice, the positioning of the defender prior to lifting the assailant will take about one second.) Lift the assailant onto your back and hip area by lifting with your knees. Pull the assailant in a counterclockwise direction for the throw.

TWO-HANDED CHOKE HOLD FROM FRONT

When the assailant is holding onto your throat, there will be sufficient room to place the fingers of your left hand into the palm area of the assailant's hand. Your fingers will be positioned over the thumb and reaching into his palm near the wrist. At the same time, place your left thumb on the back of his hand. Add the right hand to the hold by placing the right thumb on the back of the hand and allowing the fingers inside their palm to overlap the fingers of your left hand. Step back with the left foot and execute a left reverse lock takedown. When the assailant has fallen to the ground, execute a left front kick to the head.

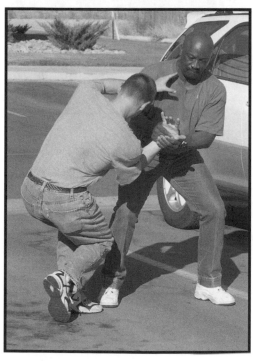

Defense Against Weapons

One of the most important goals of self-defense is to develop appropriate responses to credible threats and to respond to those threats as second nature. Each response needs to be spontaneous and able to be recalled on command, without hesitation. To be capable of that type of response, a self-defense practitioner must practice each technique correctly and repeatedly. Correct practice and repetition encourage the brain and muscle memory to develop an automatic response.

Employing a technique in a situation where an assailant has introduced a weapon requires a much greater degree of technical proficiency than defending against hand strikes and kicks. The defender must be able to recognize the weapon immediately, and then must possess the expertise to safely disarm the assailant and render him or her incapable of any further acts of aggression. These techniques typically involve the use of deadly force to save the defender or someone else from an immediate threat of death or great bodily harm. A defender who is unsure about his or her ability to use deadly force should not employ these defensive techniques and should instead allow the armed assailant to do what they came to do and leave. Defenders who choose to utilize these techniques recognize their life-saving application and employ them only as a last resort.

The techniques described in this section involve two main themes: first, disarming the assailant, and second, stopping the assailant from causing immediate or further physical harm to the defender. Although the techniques depict the disarming moves and initial follow-up, apply any additional techniques that are appropriate in the particular situation to render the assailant incapable of further attack.

For ease of explanation, the descriptions of the techniques depict the assailant presenting the weapon with the right hand. To gain the most from these techniques, first practice them with the side of the body indicated in the descriptions. After gaining proficiency on that side, reverse the technique so that it counters an assailant presenting the weapon with the left hand. This involves simply substituting left for right and vice versa.

KNIFE STAB INTO TORSO

The assailant is stabbing the defender in the abdomen with a knife. Use a left palm block to guide the knife to your right side, and catch the wrist of the knife hand with the right and left hands. Step across with the left foot and position your left shoulder toward the assailant. With both hands, move the assailant's right arm to the top of your left shoulder, with the assailant's elbow (arm turned so palm faces up) touching the shoulder. Pull down on the assailant's wrist to break the elbow. Disarm the assailant using the left hand. Move the left foot again to face the assailant. Execute a right knife hand strike to the assailant's throat.

KNIFE HELD AT NECK/THROAT

The assailant holds a knife against the left side of the defender's neck. Place the right palm on the assailant's right wrist and the left palm on the assailant's right elbow area. Press both hands inward on the assailant's right arm. By keeping equal pressure on the assailant's right elbow and wrist, force the arm to your right side at approximately waist level, being sure to keep it horizontal with the assailant bending forward at the waist (arm bar position). Quickly snap the arm by moving the wrist upward and the elbow downward, breaking the assailant's right elbow. With the left hand, disarm the assailant by prying the knife free through the assailant's fingers. If the assailant has not fallen at this point, use the left foot to sweep the assailant's right foot so he or she falls face forward. Perform a left stomp kick to the back of the head to cause loss of consciousness.

CLUB STRIKE WITH BACKHAND MOTION

While standing in front of the defender and leading with the right foot, the assailant begins to strike in a backhand motion. Begin with a right side kick to the outside of the knee of the assailant's forward leg, and block the incoming strike at the wrist with a right outer forearm block. Place the assailant in an arm bar position. Disarm the assailant by reaching with the left hand underneath the assailant's right arm. Follow immediately with a right inverted knife hand strike to the throat.

CLUB STRIKE TO THE HEAD

The assailant approaches with a tire iron or club and attempts a right overhand and downward strike to the head. Move to the right and execute a left outer forearm block. Execute a right leg takedown, followed immediately by a right knife hand strike into the assailant's throat. Disarm the assailant.

HANDGUN

The assailant holds a handgun to the defender's front torso. Use the left palm to move the gun across the assailant's body, moving the gun to your right side so you are out of the line of fire. Use the right hand to disarm the assailant and execute a right side kick to the knee. Take at least two steps away from the assailant and be prepared to use deadly force if the threat persists.

LONG GUN (SHOTGUN, ASSAULT RIFLE)

The assailant holds the weapon with the right hand nearest the trigger and the left hand closest to the barrel. Move the left foot 90 degrees to the left while simultaneously placing your right hand alongside the barrel in a downward block fashion. With the right hand, grab the barrel. Reach in with the left hand and grab the weapon at the receiver, on top and near the trigger. (The receiver of a long gun is the portion of the weapon approximately four inches to the rear of the trigger) With both hands firmly in place, deploy a right front kick to the lower torso area to soften the assailant's grasp on the weapon. Disarm the assailant in a circular figure 8 motion, beginning in the middle of the 8 and moving counterclockwise toward the top. Once the barrel reaches the top of the figure 8, the right hand will move the barrel sharply toward the assailant's face while the left hand will move just as sharply, prying through the assailant's right hand grip on the receiver. Step back with the left foot to gain distance from the assailant and prepare to use deadly force should the threat persist.

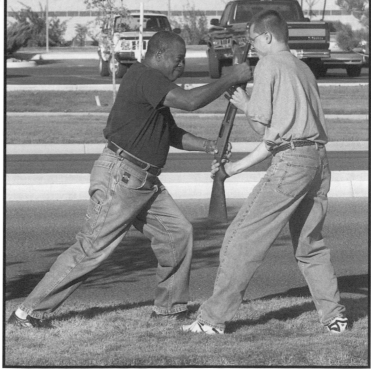

9

TACTICS FOR STREET SITUATIONS

Consider the following situations where knowledge of self-defense would be extremely beneficial.

- A woman is walking to her car at a shopping mall when she is approached by a man holding a gun. The gun-wielding man tells the woman to come with him or he will shoot her.

- A man is driving down a city street and stops behind several cars at a stoplight. A group of men approach the car, open the driver's side door, and demand that the man get out of his car and give them the keys.

- On an airplane, an apparently crazed passenger rushes up to the cockpit door and begins banging on it, attempting to gain entry.

All these situations, and many more like them, occur with frequency in cities throughout the country, with a variety of consequences. One way to increase personal safety is to recognize how these situations and crimes occur and learn the appropriate actions to take to effectively defend against them. In this chapter, we'll look at some of the violent acts that criminals perpetrate against unsuspecting victims and recommend ways to emerge from life-threatening encounters as safely as possible.

KIDNAPPING

One ploy that criminals use in abductions is to approach the victim, produce a weapon (typically a gun or a knife), and demand that the victim go with them. If a vehicle is involved, the offender either verbally or physically attempts to force the victim into the vehicle. Never voluntarily get into a vehicle, even if the offender has a weapon. There are no known cases where a victim who refused to go with an abductor was shot or stabbed on the scene. As soon as a victim gets into a vehicle, the chances of survival decrease. Refusing to get into the vehicle significantly increases the chance of survival.

The suspect may even be so bold as to attempt this crime in a public place such as a park or busy shopping center. If an assailant attempts an abduction in a public place where other people can easily observe the situation, *never* go with the offender, even if he or she has a weapon.

The criminal may choose to approach the potential victim and begin a casual conversation, perhaps by asking for the time, change, or directions. This guise, known as a confidence approach, is simply to lull the victim into a false sense of security while allowing the assailant to move closer to the victim. Criminals who use this approach depend on their skills at being able to get close to their victims. As discussed earlier, there are two distances to be concerned about: the safety zone and critical distance. If the victim feels compelled to converse with a potential criminal, the victim (defender) should keep the person inside the safety zone. If the criminal closes the distance from the safety zone using a confidence approach, it will typically be done in a manner that allows the victim to believe they are maintaining their comfort and there is no potential threat. Once inside the victim's comfort zone (which is inside the victim's critical distance), the criminal will spring their trap and attack the victim. We tell children never to talk to strangers. Perhaps if adults feel compelled to talk with strangers, the potential criminal should be kept at a safe distance.

An assailant may elect to blitz the victim in an attack without warning. The defender usually does not see the attack coming but still needs to respond to it. The average time it takes to react to a surprise is only three quarters of a second. The assailant will either produce a weapon or strike the victim with hands or feet. Refer to the sections of this book that address defenses against hand strikes, kicks, holds, and weapons.

If an assailant attempts an abduction inside a business, draw attention to the situation by knocking things off shelves or talking very loudly. The kidnapper does not want to draw attention and may elect to leave without the victim. Inside a grocery or convenience store, another place to draw attention is directly behind the counter near the cash register. Go there if you can. Get the clerk's immediate attention and demand that the police be summoned. The assailant is likely to leave without the victim. If the assailant does leave, stay in a safe location until the police arrive, and report the incident immediately.

Most criminals will not give too much thought to where they and their victims traverse and in some cases will expose themselves to surveillance cameras. These cameras help to piece together the chronology of the crime and possibly enable police to identify the suspect(s) after the crime has been committed.

Learn where surveillance cameras have been installed and are in active use. Most financial institutions, automatic teller machines, and convenience stores have active cameras. Know these general locations, and if given the opportunity, use these cameras to record the date, time, and suspect(s) involved in the incident.

If the crime has moved to a vehicle, the victim will have different roles depending on whether he or she is the driver or the passenger of that vehicle. When the assailant is the driver, plan the best moment to violently attack by gouging the eyes with the fingers or biting the face to make the assailant temporarily lose control of the vehicle and cause an accident. The best opportunities occur when the assailant is driving at a slower speed or attempting to turn corners, or when several other vehicles are present and the occupants of those vehicles can serve as witnesses. A slow-speed crash attracts attention to the vehicle and leaves evidence at the scene of the crash. The assailant will be incapable of simultaneously fending off the victim, maintaining control of the vehicle, and making a getaway. A vehicle that is disabled to the point that it cannot easily be driven away will hamper the abductor's ability to use that particular vehicle in the getaway. When the vehicle is forced to stop, the victim may be able to escape from the vehicle.

Remember that criminals take their victims to secluded places. Being around people offers a higher potential for escaping and involving others in the escape.

When the victim is the driver, select an opportunity to draw attention to the vehicle. The victim typically is familiar with the locale in which the abduction takes place and will know which areas have the largest numbers of people who may be able to help in some way. Look for law enforcement officers, fire department vehicles, taxicabs, and towtrucks that could either intervene in this situation or use their radios to call the proper authorities. Contrary to some beliefs, never drive the vehicle at *high speed* with the intent of crashing into an object. A high-speed crash may stop the abduction, but it might also have deadly results in which neither the suspect nor the victim comes out alive.

If the assailant puts the victim inside the vehicle's trunk, draw attention to the vehicle by disconnecting wires to the tail lights and brake lights and kicking out the components. The victim may not be able to see inside the dark trunk and will need to feel around for the brake and taillight wiring. After finding that wiring, pull the wires to disconnect them. Kicking out the components may allow the victim to see outside or to place an arm or leg through the hole to signal for help.

If the victim is still inside the trunk when law enforcement agents stop the vehicle, this is the time to attract attention by yelling, screaming, or kicking or striking the inside of the trunk. Keep thinking, creating, and developing escape and resistance strategies. Once you have a plan, don't be afraid to put it into action.

Hostage Situations

Criminals take hostages in a variety of scenarios: crimes that don't go according to plan, political situations, and so on. If law enforcement is summoned to a hostage scene, allow the officers to do their jobs. Most law enforcement agencies have hostage negotiators who respond to these types of incidents. They calmly establish a dialog with the hostage taker and work toward resolving the incident without further violence.

When someone is taken hostage and there are other people present, everyone there represents an immediate threat to the hostage taker, especially those who appear to be between the hostage taker and their avenue of escape. If the hostage taker has a gun, do not do anything to stop him or her from leaving unless the hostage is a loved one and the defender is mentally and physically prepared to intervene. If law enforcement officials have not yet arrived and intervention is required, one of the best things to do is to negotiate. The longer the hostage taker remains at that location with the hostage and law enforcement officials have been notified, the better the chance of the situation being resolved peacefully.

If you are negotiating with a hostage taker and someone else is the hostage, do nothing that appears to be threatening to the hostage taker. Keep at a safe distance and attempt to find out their demands. Stall for time (as you await the arrival of law enforcement officials) and comply with whatever "reasonable" demands the hostage taker makes. Do whatever is safely possible to keep them both on scene.

If the hostage taker begins to relate a series of emotional issues that require the problems being broken into smaller issues that can be addressed, this is where prior training will come into place. There are classes on conflict management that assist in learning how to break down these huge problems into smaller, more manageable problems.

If the hostage is the only person present, remember that going away with the hostage taker significantly reduces the chance of surviving this event. If negotiating is the only alternative, do not debate issues that will inflame the hostage taker. Do and say whatever is appropriate until the best moment to take defensive measures. The ultimate goal is to survive.

A person who is taken hostage may need to initially cooperate and keep silent. The longer the incident goes on, the more likely it is that the assailant will treat the hostage as an object and to some extent will forget that the hostage is a real person. The assailant will be unable to maintain the intensity of a physical hold on the victim over a prolonged time and will ultimately loosen their grip. By talking, the hostage will remind the assailant that the hostage is a real person in this situation, and the assailant will tighten his or her grip or subject the hostage to pain.

If the assailant begins to remove the hostage from the scene when law enforcement is present, the officers may resort to deadly force to immediately resolve this situation. If law enforcement is not present, two physical techniques will allow the hostage to take physical control of the situation. Each of these situations represents a worst-case scenario in which the hostage must take immediate action to preserve his or her own life.

ASSAILANT'S GUN HAND EXTENDED OUTWARD

Reach up with both hands and grab the wrist of the gun hand. Rotate the assailant's palm upward and break the assailant's elbow over your shoulder. Disarm the assailant. Shoot or otherwise disable the assailant.

GUN HAND POINTED AT HEAD

With the right shoulder free and the gun pointed at the right side of the head, move the right shoulder upward. Keeping contact with the assailant's gun hand, spin clockwise and place the assailant into a right arm bar position. Break the right elbow and disarm the assailant. Shoot or otherwise disable the assailant.

In both the preceding hostage rescue techniques, the last step calls for shooting the hostage taker. In such close quarters, failure to take immediate action may result in the assailant regaining control of the weapon after being disarmed. Also, criminals can carry more than one gun. The window of opportunity to take immediate live-saving action is very narrow. Once the defender has made the decision to use a life-saving technique, there is no room for error.

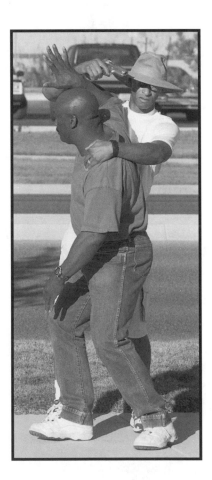

Car Jacking

Assailants car jack vehicles for a variety of reasons, ranging from escaping a crime scene to thrill seeking. In the unlikely event that an assailant attempts this crime, the only reason not to give over the vehicle is if a loved one is inside and cannot immediately escape by his or her own power. If this is the case, tell the assailant you will hand over the vehicle as soon as those inside can be removed. Be adamant about this; the lives of those still inside the vehicle may depend on it! If the answer to that demand is no, the only choice is to consider other resistance alternatives and techniques that involve immediate deadly force. These techniques were outlined in chapter 8. Take whatever action is necessary to ensure the safety of every innocent person involved. Those options may include attempting to negotiate with the suspect or employing physical defensive actions. If the assailant gets inside the car with the victim, the victim is now in a kidnapping situation and, if capable, should initiate the techniques and tactics described previously.

Air Rage

Unlike road rage, air rage is a relatively new phenomenon. Before the terrorist attacks of September 11, 2001, an air rage assailant was typically either someone with a mental disorder who was experiencing some type of psychotic episode, or an intoxicated passenger who became unruly. Although airline security has improved, incidents still occur where assailants create disturbances while an aircraft is in flight and attempt to crash through the cockpit door, threatening passengers' lives and safety.

Airline employees and other government officials (Federal Air Marshals) are responsible for the safety of the aircraft and its passengers when the aircraft is in flight and in fact may be on board. If an incident occurs and time allows, first attempt to determine if those people designated for the security issues are dealing with the situation. Secondly, check with flight attendants to determine if they require further assis-

tance. If possible, allow these professionals to do their jobs and follow their lead. If this is a worst-case scenario where time is critical or lives will be lost, this technique will render the assailant unconscious.

This technique is called the "carotid control." This move restricts the blood flow of oxygenated blood into the brain, causing the brain to overheat. This overheating results in the loss of consciousness.

It is critical that the assailant's chin is directly in line with the defender's left elbow, and that the left arm is on the assailant's throat. This will ensure the hold is in the proper position. By applying pressure on both the carotid arteries, located on the side and front of the throat, the assailant will lose consciousness.

The assailant will be unconscious from 10 to 30 seconds, depending on if the assailant is under the influence of a drug. This time period should allow the assailant to be restrained with conventional handcuffs. If handcuffs are not available, other improvised items may be used. These items consist of but are not limited to plastic flex cuffs, rope, seat belt material, neckties, belts, or anything that can bind the assailant with his or her hands behind their back. Once the assailant is properly secured, at least two people should stand guard to ensure the assailant remains secured.

- Approach the assailant from behind.
- Place the left arm around the assailant's neck, with the bend of the left elbow directly in front of the assailant's throat (the arm will be in a V shape).
- Place your left palm on top of your right biceps.

- Place your right palm on the back of the assailant's head. Tuck your face into your right biceps area (this keeps the face and eyes safe from the assailant's strikes).

- Apply pressure by flexing (squeezing together) the muscles of the left biceps and forearm on the sides of the assailant's throat.

- Walk the assailant backward to a seated position.

- Keep applying pressure with the left biceps and forearm until the assailant is rendered unconscious, which usually takes from 5 to 15 seconds.

ROAD RAGE

Road rage is aggressive driving behavior that results in some type of verbal or physical altercation. Road rage has caused numerous traffic-related incidents and altercations where the participants have sustained serious injury and death. A typical scenario for road rage is when a driver

When encountering a driver with road rage, it is best to avoid reacting angrily.

interprets an action by another driver as inappropriate and overtly expresses his or her disgust by driving recklessly or exhibiting threatening behavior toward the other driver. In such a situation, do not add fuel to the fire by expressing disgust toward the aggressive driver. If the assailant decides to yell, curse, or display the middle finger, let it happen, and do not do anything to further enrage the assailant.

Never stop and get out of the vehicle to confront the other driver, even if the other driver stops first under the guise of having a "conversation." The assailant will interpret this as an invitation to a fight. When dealing with road rage, employ escape and de-escalation tactics. If the assailant passes you, don't follow. If you are being followed, never go directly to your intended destination. Instead, drive to a busy, well-lighted area such as a hospital emergency room parking lot, a convenience store parking lot, or a police station that is open and staffed 24 hours. Once at that location, take whatever actions that provide the best chance for safety.

RESIDENTIAL BURGLARY

Today's burglars carry weapons and commit a host of other crimes, including murder. There are at least two types of burglars: those who wait until a house is unoccupied to break in, and those who prefer to break in when they know the occupants are at home.

If you ever return home only to notice that someone has burglarized the residence, it is best to retreat from the home and summon police. The criminal may still be in the act of burglarizing the home. Most burglars prefer to make their escape rather than confront the resident. However, in some cases burglars choose that opportunity to commit another crime, one of violence against one or more persons. Wait for the police to arrive and let them thoroughly check the residence to ensure the suspect(s) have left the scene. Stay outside the residence at a safe distance while the officers perform this function. Resist the temptation to go inside and search through the residence with the police. Once the residence is declared safe, take inventory to see what the criminals have taken, and file a crime report.

A *hot prowl* is when a suspect enters an occupied residence to commit a burglary when the occupants are at home and asleep. A criminal who does this poses a serious threat to personal safety because the risk of confrontation between the residents and the suspect is extremely high. During a hot prowl burglary, the first priority is to make certain that loved ones inside the home are immediately safe from harm. If possible, escape from the home and the assailant. Consider setting up a *safe room* inside your house that can serve as a refuge. That place could be any room: a bathroom, a bedroom, or a closet. A solid-core door that can be locked and bolted from the inside adds extra security. If escape from the home is not an option, sequester the entire family in the safe room.

Inside that room, keep a cellular telephone and a firearm in a quick entry gun safe to use in the event that the assailant breaks through this defensive barrier. Place the weapon at the ready and summon police assistance. Do not shoot through doors or walls at a suspect who cannot be seen. In some cases a homeowner who thinks he or she is shooting at the suspect is actually shooting at the police.

Communicate to the 9-1-1 operator the exact location of the safe room and, most importantly, the fact that the homeowner is armed inside this safe room. Do not hang up the phone! Keep the operator on the line and relay any updated information. 9-1-1 calls are tape-recorded and can serve as an accurate record of what transpired from the time the call was received.

Stay in the safe room until the police arrive to make a rescue. Do not leave the safe room to let the police in. If the police need to get inside the residence, they will be resourceful enough to find a way. If necessary, they can break open a door or a window to gain access to the residence.

Never leave the safe room to confront the suspect and attempt to hold him or her for the police. The family's personal safety is much more important than attempting to catch a burglar. Let the police do their jobs, even at the risk of the suspect escaping from the home and eluding the police.

HOME INVASION

Home invasions are robberies or other violent crimes that occur inside the home, usually when the occupants are awake. The suspects either force a door open or knock first and then force their way in once the resident opens the door. Some options exist to deter a criminal from ever targeting a residence in the first place.

- A reliable alarm system that includes interior and exterior sirens as well as perimeter sensors and motion sensors. When a home is properly equipped with an alarm system, display signs to that effect in the front, side, and rear windows of the residence. Ideally, this type of "target hardening" will deter criminals from entering this home and send them instead to a home without an alarm system.

- A dog to protect its masters. A deterrent to being targeted is having a large dog that is psychologically intimidating to the intruder and will attack if provoked. Some breeds are naturally inclined to protect their masters and are only too happy to perform that task, while other breeds may look cute but provide no master-protection qualities. Some breeds that naturally offer master protection are German Shepherds and Dobermans.

Gimmicks such as the fake dog alarm that "barks" when someone knocks on the door do not work. Also, do not depend on Beware of Dog signs or large dog dishes at the front door to warn people about a nonexistent dog. Criminals usually see through the guise and break in anyway.

- A peephole in the door. Whenever someone knocks on the door, look through the peephole to confirm their identity. If the person was not invited or their identity is in question, do not open the door, no matter what they are selling or saying. Never allow anyone to talk their way into the home. No means no! If someone does not want to take no for an answer, call 9-1-1 to summon police.

- A home-invasion plan. Develop a plan to use if someone comes into the home uninvited. Although the defender should summon the police via 9-1-1 as soon as the uninvited guest has forced his or her way inside, remember that it will take the police several minutes to arrive. In some places throughout the nation, emergency 9-1-1 systems are overtaxed, and callers are sometimes placed on hold.

One of the best options for self-defense may be to take refuge inside a safe room. To access this safe room, the resident needs to recognize that his or her home is being invaded and must take action before the suspect(s) have completed their entry into the home. If children are inside the residence take all loved ones into the safe room and secure the door, locking out the intruder. Another option is to escape from the intruder by leaving the home. If physically attacked while inside the home, take whatever action is necessary to survive the attack. The best option is to escape; the second-best option is to use de-escalation skills; however, be prepared to take physical action if de-escalation skills do not succeed. Last, the defender may have to physically resist the attacker, but only if the defender is fully capable of defending against the attack.

In some cases, criminals spot potential victims at a different location and then follow them home, where the attack occurs. Be cautious while traveling home from other places. Take different routes each day and periodically check to see if anyone is following you. Teach family members and other residents of the home to do likewise.

People have been attacked as they take out the trash, pick up the mail, or carry laundry or other items to or from their homes. Be prepared for an attack coming from anywhere, at any time. If attacked, drop any items that are expendable to either make an escape or employ a resistance technique.

STREET GANG ENCOUNTERS

Criminal gangs plague many of today's cities. Whether they are driven by turf disputes, drugs, or racial hatred, gangs have infected the fabric of society. Knowing that these gangs exist within most cities will enable the defender to be aware of areas to avoid. Local law enforcement agencies can provide information as to the particular gangs that operate in a city and the turf they claim.

Historically, street gangs tend to target and victimize their rival street gangs. Innocent people, however, sometimes are caught in the middle of violent gang warfare.

When dealing with gangs or gang members, it may be best to employ escape and de-escalation tactics. Remember, many gang members are likely to be present. Because of the number of assailants and their propensity to inflict extreme levels of violence, only as a last resort should a defender employ physical techniques.

Random Violence

Violence can erupt anywhere, in public or in private. It can take the form of an armed robbery, a drive-by shooting, workplace violence, a domestic murder in a public place, a terrorist attack, or a police shootout. Violent acts can occur in fast-food restaurants, grocery stores, and tourist attractions. In recent years, random acts of violence have also taken place in schools, churches, and airports. Discuss self-defense options with family members so everyone knows what to do if this type of emergency arises.

Whenever you are in a public place, make it a habit to know exactly where all the exits and escape routes are located. Plan a course of action that incorporates several escape routes and potential hiding places. Always position yourself in a way that lets you see everyone who enters the area. If a random act of violence erupts, consider the following tactics:

1. **Escape.** This tactic provides the best chance for safety. More often than not, an offender will attempt to kill only the intended person(s); however, he or she may randomly seek innocent people. Sometimes unintended victims are also caught in the crossfire.

Consider conventional escape routes such as doors, hallways, and stairways that can be accessed in an emergency. Do not forget about unconventional escape tactics such as breaking a window, creating a door by breaking through drywall, or using a makeshift ladder to crawl to safety.

2. **Cover.** If immediate escape is impossible, look for objects that offer the best protection against bullets, such as brick walls, engine block areas in vehicles, and building exteriors. After reaching this initial place of cover, escape to a safer place at the earliest opportunity.

3. **Submission.** Acquiescing to the offender means placing innocent lives in the criminal's hands. Submission can come in the form of being cooperative with the demands of the offender, becoming a hostage, or in the case of a shooting, playing dead. Physical resistance against an armed offender who has the present ability to use deadly force is extremely dangerous; use it as a last resort to save lives. Keep in mind that giving in to an armed offender places him or her in complete control. In law enforcement academies and other related training seminars throughout the nation, officers are taught to never give in to an armed offender. If the officer or defender must submit to the offender, it is only temporary until other measures can be taken to defeat the offender.

Riots

In a riot, the crowd is often overcome by a mob mentality and attacks just about anyone who is present. The acts perpetrated are often senselessly

Don't stand around and watch a riot escalate. Leave the area as quickly as you can.

violent and can lead to death. If caught in a riot, *immediately* escape from the affected areas. Never become a spectator of a riot. Many innocent people have become riot victims when all they wanted to do was watch the scene unfold.

As you escape, you may or may not have an opportunity to take your immediate personal property. Personal property such as your vehicle or the goods inside your vehicle (wallet, purse, other valuables) may not be safe to collect. If you are inside a business or residence and within the affected area and need to escape, do not take time to obtain valuables or collectibles that have sentimental value. It's better to escape with lives intact. Once law enforcement officials have deemed it safe to return, only then should you return and determine the status of the personal property left behind. In a situation involving a riot or any large and unruly crowd, it's best to employ escape tactics. Use physical techniques only as a last resort because of the number of participants and extreme level of violence that may be involved.

ROBBERY

Criminals who commit robberies typically just want the property they are after and many times do not harm their victims. Robberies can be committed with or without a weapon. A criminal who does not use a weapon of deadly force (a gun, a knife, or an improvised weapon such as a rock or stick) may elect to use violence by striking with the hands or feet or threatening to use a weapon. Don't be a hero by trying to take the person into custody, getting into a fight over the property, or chasing after the suspect to retrieve the property or to catch him or her for the police.

When confronted by a criminal who wants to commit a robbery and no immediate bodily harm is taking place, hand over the tangible goods and allow the criminal to leave the area. If the criminal is physically attacking and causing physical harm, do everything possible to stop the attack.

Never allow a criminal to tie up, bind, or in any other way physically restrict the movements of the defender. Binding reduces the victim's chances of survival. No one can adequately defend themselves when tied up. Refer to the chapters on defending against hand strikes, kicks, and weapons and breaking holds.

STALKING

A stalker is defined as a person without lawful authority who willfully or maliciously engages in a course of conduct that causes a reasonable person to feel terrorized, frightened, intimidated, or harassed. In today's society, men as well as women are viable targets for stalkers. A stalker can be someone who had a former relationship with the victim or someone totally unknown.

Stalking severely affects the victim's life as well as the lives of everyone associated with the victim. There are a number of things a stalking victim can do, including taking legal and proactive steps to increase personal safety and filing a police report with the local law enforcement agency to document the offense.

The victim will also need to notify his or her family, close friends, and co-workers about the incident(s) in case they come into contact with the stalker. These people may not need to know all the intricate details, but just enough facts to keep them informed and alert.

If you know the identity of the suspect, seek a restraining order against him or her. Obtain a photograph of the suspect and provide copies to co-workers, work supervisors, and immediate family. The photo will help others immediately recognize the suspect should he or she approach a particular location.

Keep a very detailed account or diary of each contact with the stalker as well as any suspicious circumstances, even though some events may not make sense at the time they occur. They may later be attributed to the stalker as more facts are unraveled. Include in your written statement for the police report that you are keeping a diary, and specify its location should an untimely event prevent you from retrieving the diary at a later date.

Last, consider the use of personal weapons. If choosing a weapon that has the capacity to take a human life, be prepared legally, mentally, and physically to use deadly force if the situation calls for it. Once prepared, do not hesitate if the time comes. If you are not prepared to use the weapon, the stalker may disarm you and use your own weapon against you.

BE A GOOD WITNESS

If you see a crime occur, unless special training, equipment, and all other factors are in your favor, do not get directly involved. Instead, be a good witness. By remaining safe, either at the scene or at another safe location, observe the crime and summon law enforcement. In some cases a bystander observes a crime and gets directly involved by coming to the victim's aid. Although getting physically involved can work out for the best, sometimes the rescuer becomes the target of the criminal's aggression and needs to be rescued as well.

If your family members are present, it is best not to get directly involved. Consider that they might be forced to watch their worst nightmare come true—you being seriously being hurt or killed while the criminal commits violent acts.

AFTER AN ALTERCATION

After deploying the physical technique, a defender has absolutely no need to hold or attempt to hold onto the assailant to ensure that he or she is arrested for their act(s) of aggression. The law requires on-duty law enforcement officers to apprehend and control violent offenders. Officers usually wear uniforms or some other item that clearly identifies them as law enforcement personnel. They will have a host of equipment to assist them in the process of restraining offenders—body armor, handcuffs, a radio to call for assistance, and a firearm for protection. These officers will also have the necessary training in physical and psychological tactics to control and restrain violent offenders. Private citizens have no legal obligation to restrain the assailant after an altercation so that he or she may face the legal consequences of their actions. Attempting to restrain an assailant for the police is extremely dangerous and should be avoided at all costs.

If the assailant is attempting to escape, allow him or her to leave the scene as long as the escape creates no further threat to human life. Preservation of human life is always the most important consideration. Insurance companies can compensate for property losses but can never repay the cost of a human life. Allow the assailant to flee if that creates a safer environment for the defender.

After any physical altercation, immediately leave the scene and go to a safe area. Remaining on the scene only increases the chances of a subsequent altercation with the assailant or the assailant's friends or family. In countless cases, assailants or their friends or family members have either initiated another attack on the defender or have returned after the altercation with weapons to use on the defender for retribution. In some cases, people have even driven their vehicles through buildings in an attempt to "get even."

If it is necessary to summon the police or emergency medical services, go to a safe place and call to report what occurred. You have no legal requirement to stay at an unsafe location to report a crime or to stay on the scene and summon aid for someone who is injured as a result of their criminal actions. Always go to a safe place and summon whatever assistance is needed from there.

It's always a good idea to report the incident to a law enforcement agency. Reporting the incident accomplishes several things:

- It advises the people who are charged with public safety that this incident occurred.
- It documents the identity of the people involved in the incident.
- It ensures that medical assistance will be provided to those who may require it at the scene of the incident.
- It lets law enforcement personnel know that the defender is willing to cooperate in any subsequent investigation of the incident.

After notifying law enforcement of the altercation, carefully check for any substantial injuries to your body. The human body's natural reaction to danger causes the adrenal glands to prepare the body for combat. This preparation sometimes blocks the body's response to pain, and as a result the defender may not be aware of the magnitude of injury sustained during the altercation, or even that an injury took place at all.

As soon as possible, and in a safe environment, take a physical inventory of your body. Look for any signs of external injuries, however slight. If any blood is present, check where it is coming from to verify if it belongs to the defender or to the assailant. Often, a defender sees a large amount of blood on the body and initially thinks it is from the assailant. Once the adrenal glands stop supplying adrenaline, however, the defender discovers he or she has sustained a major injury that requires immediate emergency medical treatment. If you find any significant injuries, immediately summon emergency medical services.

Internal injuries are much more difficult to verify. After the altercation, these injuries may manifest themselves in any number of ways, from blood in the urine to a host of other symptoms. Again, once the adrenaline stops flowing, most injuries will reveal themselves. The defender may feel sore in one or more areas of the body, indicating the location and nature of the injury. If any of these symptoms are present, seek medical attention.

Conclusion

People who participate in self-defense programs are motivated by the desire to protect themselves and their loved ones. When practicing self-defense, pay strict attention to detail. The form of each movement is critical; without proper form, the movements will not flow well. Focus pertains to striking a particular target with 100 percent accuracy.

Inaccurate strikes will not have the desired effect on the assailant and will allow the fight to continue longer than necessary. The longer the fight continues, the greater the likelihood of injury to the defender.

Emulate all of the movements depicted in the photographs of each technique. After accuracy in form, the next most important element is the timing of each movement. A practice partner can assist in developing proper timing of each block and strike. After gaining proficiency in these defensive movements, add speed to the defensive strikes. Ultimately, the defender will be capable of defending against a full-speed attack while executing the defensive technique with form, focus, and control.

Self-defense can be very fun and exciting as the defender rises to the challenge of mastering new movements. With sufficient practice, the movements can be used in actual combat, and the results can be extremely rewarding. Take the time to do it right.

INDEX

pectoral strike, with simultaneous block, as
        hand strike defense 79, 79f
peephole, as home defense 170
pepper spray 12-13, 13f
"perception-reaction" mode 9
personal defense. *See* self-defense
personal property
        home as. *See* home environment
        during street situations 173-175
        theft of. *See* robbery
physical fitness
        as assailants' advantage 20
        conditioning for 25-30
        requirements for 2-3, 25
physical signs, of an attack 46-48
physical speed 111
physical tactics 7, 17, 45
physician input, for physical conditioning
        25
physiology, of aggression 44, 176
police, in street situations 159-161, 169-
        172, 175
        summoning 175-176
positioning
        of assailant 45-46
        with hand strikes 51
        with kicking 103-104, 106
power, developing for kicks 47, 111, 113
power punches. *See* punches
practice sessions. *See also specific*
        technique
        importance of 44, 177
        safety in 4
preconceived notions, impact on mental
        readiness 14-15
prelude(s)
        to escape 18-19
        to imminent attacks 10-12
preoccupation, as mental error 23, 29
pressure, applying for restraint 167-168
prevention, as weapons defense 148
property losses
        personal 173-175
        residential 169-171
psychological challenges, of self-defense 2,
        19-21
punches. *See also* hand strikes
        critical distance for 50-51, 118
        developing specific movements for
                51-58
        hand combinations for 59-60
        kicks for beating
                quadruple 74, 75f
                triple combination 92, 92f-93f
        physical signs preceding 46-47

target areas for 49-50, 61-62
punch-timing drill 62

Q
quadruple kick, beating the punch with 74,
        75f

R
rage, defense tactics for
        in the air 166-168
        on the road 168-169
random violence, defense tactics for 172
rapid front punch, as hand combination 60
reaction, as self-defense mode 9-10
        avoidance with road rage 168-169
rehearsal, of attacks, competency through
        4, 15, 20-21
relaxing, as mental error 23
repetitions
        for warm-up 26
        for workout 29-30, 44
replacement theory, for hand strikes 59
reporting, of incidents 176
rescue techniques
        for hostage situations 161-162
                armed 162, 162f-165f, 164
        for kidnapping 159-161
residential burglary, defense tactics for
        169-170
        invasive 170-171
resistance, as self-defense
        with home invasion 170-171
        for kidnapping 159-161
restraining order, for stalking 174
restraint
        as air rage defense 166-168, 167f
        legal obligation for 175
        victim's avoidance of 174
retribution, in modern fights 2
reverse motions, as hand strike defense 64,
        64f-65f
reverse wrist lock, with takedown, as hand
        and foot strike defense 98,
        98f-99f
rib strike, as hand strike defense
        with lateral movements 100-102,
                101f
        and takedown after X block 78, 78f
right hand strikes 49-50, 62
        lateral movement defense technique
                for 100-102, 101f
right leg kicks 106, 114-115
riots, defense tactics for 172-173, 173f
rising block 32-33, 32f
road rage, defense tactics for 168-169

stun guns 12-13, 13*f*
submission, as random violence defense 172
substitutions, in movements and technique 62
summoning assistance, from the law 175-176
surveillance cameras 160
survival, as most important result in attacks 24, 175
sweep. *See* foot sweep

T
tactics, for self-defense strikes 7, 39, 45
takedown
    after X block and rib strike, as hand strike defense 78, 78*f*
    as kick defense
        with cross-body block and groin stomp 134, 134*f*-135*f*
        knee rollover 136, 136*f*-137*f*
        knee wrench 138, 138*f*-139*f*
    with palm strike to face, as hand strike defense 67, 67f
    reverse wrist lock, as hand and foot strike defense 98, 98*f*-99*f*
taps. *See* chin tap; ear tap
target area
    for kicks 103-106
    for punches 49-50, 61-62
    in self-defense strikes 7, 39, 45, 49
target hardening 5, 170
Taser® stun gun 12, 13*f*
techniques
    basic self-defense 30-44
    movements *vs.* 29-30
    real-life self-defense 44-45
    substitution of 62
threats
    credible 148, 158, 161
    in street situations 158, 169-171, 175-177
three strikes, you're out, as kick combination 115
throat, knife held at, defense against 150, 150*f*-151*f*
throat strike, elbow break and X block with, for dominant hand strike defense 88, 88*f*-89*f*
thrust kick 106
tie up. *See* restraint
timing, of self-defense strikes 7, 62
tombstone courage, as mental error 23

torso
    kicks to 105, 113-115
    knife stab into, defense against 149, 149*f*
    position, with kicking 103
    proper punches to 50
"traditional" techniques, as school focus 3-4
triple kicks 114
    combination
        beating the punch with 74, 75*f*
        block and, as kick defense 124, 124*f*-125*f*
trunks, of vehicles, kidnappings in 160-161
two-handed choke hold from front, breaking from 147, 147*f*

U
upward chin tap, armpit strike and block with, as haymaker punch defense 90, 90*f*-91*f*

V
vehicles
    jacking of, defense tactics for 166
    kidnappings with 160-161
    as weapon 176
verbal cues
    by aggressor 7-8, 10
    for de-escalation 10-11
victim
    assailant's abduction of. *See* kidnapping
    assailant's approach toward 16, 159, 171
    assailant's selection of 15-16
    comfort zone of, with kidnapping 159
    mental readiness of 16
    as self-defense element 4, 175
violence. *See* attack(s)
visualization, as defenders' advantage 20-21

W
walk on by, as kick combination 115
warm-up, for conditioning 25-26, 29
warning
    avoid giving with movements 46-47
    verbal, against imminent attack 11
weapons
    defense against
        components of 3, 6, 17-18
        techniques for 148-157

ABOUT THE AUTHOR

Joseph B. Walker is a patrol lieutenant watch commander for the Reno Police Department in Reno, Nevada. With more than 25 years of experience as a law enforcement official, Walker has served on or supervised the dignitary protection of such high-profile clients as former President Gerald Ford, Martin Luther King III, Bernice King, and baseball great Hank Aaron.

Walker has studied and taught the martial arts and self-defense since the early 1970s. A qualified personal safety specialist, he is also an eighth-degree black belt in karate and president of the Kifaru Karate Organization. He devised the school safety contingency plan for the Washoe County School District and authored the *Stalking Guide for Law Enforcement Officers* for the Reno Police Department.

Walker lives in Reno, Nevada, with his wife, Coleen. He enjoys spending time with his family, teaching and training in the martial arts, and performing music.

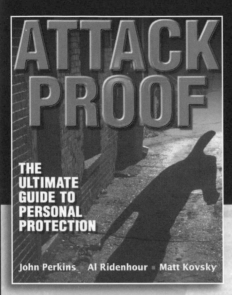